LESSONS IN TRUTH

Twelve Lessons in Practical Christianity

H. Emilie Cady

Originally published In 1896

Contents

Lesson 1

Bondage or Liberty, Which?

In entering upon this course of instruction, each of you should, so far as possible, lay aside, for the time being, all previous theories and beliefs. By so doing you will be saved the trouble of trying, all the way through the course, to put "new wine into old wineskins" (Lk. 5:37). If there is anything, as we proceed, which you do not understand or agree with, just let it lie passively in your mind until you have read the entire book, for many statements that would at first arouse antagonism and discussion will be clear and easily accepted a little farther on. After the course is completed, if you wish to return to your old beliefs and ways of living, you are at perfect liberty to do so. But, for the time being, be willing to become as a little child; for, said the Master, in spiritual things, "Except ye . . . become as little children, ye shall in no wise enter into the kingdom of heaven" (Mt. 18:3). If at times there seems to be repetition, please remember that these are lessons, not lectures.

"Finally . . be strong in the Lord, and in the strength of his might" (Eph. 6:10).

"Finally, brethren, whatsoever things are true, whatsoever things are honorable, whatsoever things are just, whatsoever things are pure, whatsoever things are lovely, whatsoever things are of good report; if there be any virtue, and if there be any praise, think on these things" (Phil. 4:8).

1. Every man believes himself to be in bondage to the flesh and to the things of the flesh. All suffering is the result of this belief. The history of the coming of the Children of

Israel out of their long bondage in Egypt is descriptive of the human mind, or consciousness, growing up out of the animal or sense part of man and into the spiritual part.

2. "And Jehovah said [speaking to Moses], I have surely seen the affliction of my people that are in Egypt, and I have heard their cry by reason of their taskmasters; for I know their sorrows;

3. "And I am come down to deliver them out of the hand of the Egyptians, and to bring them up out of that land unto a good land and a large, unto a land flowing with milk and honey" (Ex. 3:7,8).

4. These words express exactly the attitude of the Creator toward His highest creation, man.

5. Today, and all the days, He has been saying to us, His children: "I have surely seen the affliction of you who are in Egypt [darkness of ignorance], and have heard your cry by reason of your taskmasters [sickness, sorrow, and poverty]; and I am [not I will, but I am now] come down to deliver you out of all this suffering, and to bring you up unto a good land and a large, unto a land flowing with good things" (Ex. 3:7 adapted).

6. Sometime, somewhere, every human being must come to himself. Having tired of eating husks, he will "arise and go to my Father" (Lk. 15:18).

"For it is written,
As I live, saith the Lord, to me every knee shall bow,
And every tongue shall confess to God"
(Rom. 14:11).

7. This does not mean that God is a stern autocrat who by reason of supreme power compels man to bow to Him. It is rather an expression of the order of divine law, the law of all love, all good. Man, who is at first living in the selfish animal part of himself, will grow up through various stages and by various processes to the divine or spiritual understanding wherein he knows that he is one with the Father, and wherein he is free from all suffering, because he has conscious dominion over all things. Somewhere on this journey the human consciousness, or intellect, comes to a place where it gladly bows to its spiritual self and confesses that this spiritual self, its Christ, is highest and is Lord. Here and forever after, not with sense of bondage, but with joyful freedom, the heart cries out: "Jehovah reigneth" (Ps. 93:1). Everyone must sooner or later come to this point of experience.

8. You and I, dear reader, have already come to ourselves. Having become conscious of an oppressive bondage, we have arisen and set out on the journey from Egypt to the land of liberty, and now we cannot turn back if we would. Though possibly there will come times to each of us, before we reach the land of milk and honey (the time of full deliverance out of all our sorrows and troubles), when we shall come into a deep wilderness or against a seemingly impassable Red Sea, when our courage will seem to fail. Yet God says to each one of us, as Moses said to the trembling Children of Israel: "Fear ye not, stand still, and see the salvation of Jehovah, which he will work for you today" (Ex. 14:13).

9. Each man must sooner or later learn to stand alone with his God; nothing else avails. Nothing else will ever make you master of your own destiny. There is in your own indwelling Lord all the life and health, all the strength and

peace and joy, all the wisdom and support that you can ever need or desire. No one can give to you as can this indwelling Father. He is the spring of all joy and comfort and power.

10. Hitherto we have believed that we were helped and comforted by others, that we received joy from outside circumstances and surroundings; but it is not so. All joy and strength and good spring up from a fountain within one's own being; and if we only knew this truth we should know that, because God in us is the fountain out of which springs all our good, nothing that anyone does or says, or fails to do or say, can take away our joy and good.

11. Someone has said: "Our liberty comes from an understanding of the mind and the thoughts of God toward us." Does God regard man as His servant, or as His child? Most of us have believed ourselves not only the slaves of circumstances, but also, at the best, the servants of the Most High. Neither belief is true. It is time for us to awake to right thoughts, to know that we are not servants, but children, "and if children, then heirs" (Rom. 8:17). Heirs to what? Why, heirs to all wisdom, so that we need not, through any lack of wisdom, make mistakes; heirs to all love, so that we need know no fear or envy or jealousy; heirs to all strength, all life, all power, all good.

12. The human intelligence is so accustomed to the sound of words heard from childhood that often they convey to it no real meaning. Do you stop to think, really to comprehend, what it means to be "heirs of God, and joint-heirs with Christ" (Rom. 8:17)? It means, "Every man is the inlet, and may become the outlet, of all there is in God." It means that all that God is and has is in reality for us, His only heirs, if we only know how to claim our inheritance.

13. This claiming of our rightful inheritance, the inheritance that God wants us to have in our daily life, is just what we are learning how to do in these simple talks.

14. Paul said truly: "So long as the heir is a child, he differeth nothing from a bondservant though he is lord of all;

15. "But is under guardians and stewards until the day appointed of the father.

16. "So we also, when we were children [in knowledge], were held in bondage under the rudiments of the world:

17. "But when the fulness of the time came, God sent forth his Son . . . And because ye are sons, God sent forth the Spirit of his Son into our hearts [or into our conscious minds], crying Abba, Father.

18. "So that thou art no longer a bondservant but a son; and if a son, then an heir through God" (Gal. 4:1-7).

19. It is through Christ, the indwelling Christ, that we are to receive all that God has and is, as much or as little as we can or dare to claim.

20. No matter with what object you first started out to seek Truth, it was in reality because it was God's "fulness of the time" (Gal. 4:4) for you to arise and begin to claim your inheritance. You were no longer to be satisfied with or under bondage to the elements of the world. Think of it! God's "fulness of the time" now for you to be free, to have dominion over all things material, to be no longer bond servant, but a son in possession of your inheritance! "Ye

did not choose me, but I chose you, and appointed you, that ye should go and bear fruit" (Jn. 15:16).

21. We have come to a place now where our search for Truth must no longer be for the rewards; it must no longer be our seeking a creed to follow, but it must be our living a life. In these simple lessons we shall take only the first steps out of the Egyptian bondage of selfishness, lust, and sorrow toward the land of liberty, where perfect love and all good reign.

22. Every right thought that we think, our every unselfish word or action, is bound by immutable laws to be fraught with good results. But in our walk we must learn to lose sight of results that are the "loaves and the fishes" (Mt. 15:36). We must rather seek to be the Truth consciously, to be love, to be wisdom, to be life (as we really are unconsciously,) and let results take care of themselves.

23. Every man must take time daily for quiet and meditation. In daily meditation lies the secret of power. No one can grow in either spiritual knowledge or power without it. Practice the presence of God just as you would practice music. No one would ever dream of becoming a master in music except by spending some time daily alone with music. Daily meditation alone with God focuses the divine presence within us and brings it to our consciousness.

24. You may be so busy with the doing, the outgoing of love to help others (which is unselfish and Godlike as far as it goes), that you find no time to go apart. But the command, or rather the invitation, is "Come ye yourselves apart . . . and rest a while" (Mk. 6:31). And it is the only way in which you will ever gain definite knowledge, true

wisdom, newness of experience, steadiness of purpose, or power to meet the unknown, which must come in all daily life. Doing is secondary to being. When we are consciously the Truth, it will radiate from us and accomplish the works without our ever running to and fro. If you have no time for this quiet meditation, make time, take time. Watch carefully, and you will find that there are some things, even in the active unselfish doing, which would better be left undone than that you should neglect regular meditation.

25. You will find that some time is spent every day in idle conversation with people who "just run in for a few moments" to be entertained. If you can help such people, well; if not, gather yourself together and do not waste a moment idly diffusing and dissipating yourself to gratify their idleness. You have no idea what you lose by it.

26. When you withdraw from the world for meditation, let it not be to think of yourself or your failures, but invariably to get all your thoughts centered on God and on your relation to the Creator and Upholder of the universe. Let all the little annoying cares and anxieties go for a while, and by effort, if need be, turn your thoughts away from them to some of the simple words of the Nazarene, or of the Psalmist. Think of some Truth statement, be it ever so simple.

27. No person, unless he has practiced it, can know how it quiets all physical nervousness, all fear, all oversensitiveness, all the little raspings of everyday life-- just this hour of calm, quiet waiting alone with God. Never let it be an hour of bondage, but always one of restfulness.

28. Some, having realized the calm and power that come of daily meditation, have made the mistake of drawing

themselves from the world, that they may give their entire time to meditation. This is asceticism, which is neither wise nor profitable.

29. The Nazarene, who is our noblest type of the perfect life, went daily apart from the world only that He might come again into it with renewed spiritual power. So we go apart into the stillness of divine presence that we may come forth into the world of everyday life with new inspiration and increased courage and power for activity and for overcoming.

30. "We talk to God--that is prayer; God talks to us--that is inspiration." We go apart to get still, that new life, new inspiration, new power of thought, new supply from the fountainhead may flow in; and then we come forth to shed it on those around us, that they, too, may be lifted up. Inharmony cannot remain in any home where even one member of the family daily practices this hour of the presence of God, so surely does the renewed infilling of the heart by peace and harmony result in the continual outgoing of peace and harmony into the entire surroundings.

31. Again, in this new way that we have undertaken, this living the life of Spirit instead of the old self, we need to seek always to have more and more of the Christ Spirit of meekness and love incorporated into our daily life. Meekness does not mean servility, but it means a spirit that could stand before a Pilate of false accusation and say nothing. No one else is so grand, so godlike as he who, because he knows the Truth of Being, can stand meekly and unperturbed before the false accusations of the human mind. "Thy gentleness hath made me great" (2 Sam. 2:36).

32. We must forgive as we would be forgiven. To forgive does not simply mean to arrive at a place of indifference to those who do personal injury to us; it means far more than this. To forgive is to give for--to give some actual, definite good in return for evil given. One may say: "I have no one to forgive; I have not a personal enemy in the world." And yet if, under any circumstances, any kind of a "served-him-right" thought springs up within you over anything that any of God's children may do or suffer, you have not yet learned how to forgive.

33. The very pain that you suffer, the very failure to demonstrate over some matter that touches your own life deeply, may rest upon just this spirit of unforgiveness that you harbor toward the world in general. Put it away with resolution.

34. Do not be under bondage to false beliefs about your circumstances or environment. No matter how evil circumstances may appear, or how much it may seem that some other personality is at the foundation of your sorrow or trouble, God, good, good alone, is really there when you call His law into expression.

35. If we have the courage to persist in seeing only God in it all, even "the wrath of man" (Ps. 76:10) shall be invariably turned to our advantage. Joseph, in speaking of the action of his brethren in selling him into slavery, said, "As for you, ye meant evil against me; but God meant it for good" (Gen. 50:20). To them that love God, "all things work together for good" (Rom. 8:28), or to them who recognize only God. All things! The very circumstances in your life that seem heartbreaking evils will turn to joy before your very eyes if you will steadfastly refuse to see anything but God in them.

36. It is perfectly natural for the human mind to seek to escape from its troubles by running away from present environments, or by planning some change on the material plane. Such methods of escape are absolutely vain and foolish. "Vain is the help of man" (Ps. 60:11).

37. There is no permanent or real outward way of escape from miseries or circumstances; all help must come from within.

38. The words, "God is my defense and deliverance," held in the silence until they become part of your very being, will deliver you out of the hands and the arguments of the keenest lawyer in the world.

39. The real inner consciousness that "the LORD is my shepherd; I shall not want" (Ps. 23:1 A.V.) will supply all wants more surely and far more liberally than can any human hand.

40. The ultimate aim of every man should be to come into the consciousness of an indwelling God, and then in all external matters, to affirm deliverance through and by this divine One. There should not be a running to and fro, making human efforts to aid the Divine, but a calm, restful, unwavering trust in All-Wisdom and All-Power within one as able to accomplish the thing desired.

41. Victory must be won in the silence of your own being first, and then you need take no part in the outer demonstration of relief from conditions. The very walls of Jericho that keep you from your desire must fall before you.

42. The Psalmist said:

"I will lift up mine eyes unto the mountains

[or to the highest One]:

From whence shall come my help?

43. "My help cometh from Jehovah,

Who made heaven and earth.

44. "Jehovah [your indwelling Lord] will keep thee from evil . . .

45. "Jehovah will keep thy going out and thy coming in

From this time forth, and for evermore."

(Ps. 121:1, 2, 7, 8)

Lesson 2

Statement of Being

Who And What God Is

Who And What Man Is

1. When Jesus was talking with the Samaritan woman at the well, He said to her, "God is Spirit: and they that worship him must worship in spirit and truth." (John 4:24 A.V. reads, "God is a Spirit," but the marginal note is, "God is Spirit," and some other versions render this passage, "God is Spirit.") To say "a Spirit" would be to

imply the existence of more than one Spirit. Jesus, in His statement, did not imply this.

2. Webster in his definition of Spirit says: "In the abstract, life or consciousness viewed as an independent type of existence. One manifestation of the divine nature; the Holy Spirit."

3. God, then, is not, as many of us have been taught to believe, a big personage or man residing somewhere in a beautiful region in the sky, called "heaven," where good people go when they die, and see Him clothed in ineffable glory; nor is He a stern, angry judge only awaiting opportunity somewhere to punish bad people who have failed to live a perfect life here.

4. God is Spirit, or the creative energy that is the cause of all visible things. God as Spirit is the invisible life and intelligence underlying all physical things. There could be no body, or visible part, to anything unless there was first Spirit as creative cause.

5. God is not a being or person having life, intelligence, love, power. God is that invisible, intangible, but very real, something we call life. God is perfect love and infinite power. God is the total of these, the total of all good, whether manifested or unexpressed.

6. There is but one God in the universe, but one source of all the different forms of life or intelligence that we see, whether they be men, animals, trees, or rocks.

7. God is Spirit. We cannot see Spirit with these fleshly eyes; but when we clothe ourselves with the spiritual body, then Spirit is visible or manifest and we recognize it. You

do not see the living, thinking "me" when you look at my body. You see only the form which I am manifesting.

8. God is love. We cannot see love or grasp any comprehension of what love is, except as love is clothed with a form. All the love in the universe is God. The love between husband and wife, between parents and children, is just the least little bit of God, as pushed forth in visible form into manifestation. A mother's love, so infinitely tender, so unfailing, is God's love, only manifested in greater degree by the mother.

9. God is wisdom and intelligence. All the wisdom and intelligence that we see in the universe is God, is wisdom projected through a visible form. To educate (from educare, to lead forth) never means to force into from the outside, but always means to draw out from within something already existing there. God as infinite wisdom lies within every human being, only waiting to be led forth into manifestation. This is true education.

10. Heretofore we have sought knowledge and help from outside sources, not knowing that the source of all knowledge, the very Spirit of truth, is lying latent within each one of us, waiting to be called on to teach us the truth about all things--most marvelous of teachers, and everywhere present, without money or price!

11. God is power. Not simply God has power, but God is power. In other words, all the power there is to do anything is God. God, the source of our existence every moment, is not simply omnipotent (all-powerful); He is omnipotence (all power). He is not alone omniscient (all-knowing); He is omni-science (all knowledge). He is not only omni-present, but more--omnipresence. God is not a being having

qualities, but He is the good itself. Everything that you can think of that is good, when in its absolute perfection, goes to make up that invisible Being we call God.

12. God, then, is the substance (from sub, under, and stare, to stand), or the real thing standing under every visible form of life, love, intelligence, or power. Each rock, tree, animal, every visible thing, is a manifestation of the one Spirit--God--differing only in degree of manifestation; and each of the numberless modes of manifestation or individualities, however insignificant, contains the whole.

13. One drop of water taken from the ocean is just as perfect ocean water as the whole great body. The constituent elements of water are exactly the same, and they are combined in precisely the same ratio or perfect relation to each other, whether we consider one drop, a pailful, a barrelful, or the entire ocean out of which the lesser quantities are taken; each is complete in itself; they differ only in quantity or degree. Each contains the whole; and yet no one would make the mistake of supposing from this statement that each drop is the entire ocean.

14. So we say that each individual manifestation of God contains the whole; not for a moment meaning that each individual is God in His entirety, so to speak, but that each is God come forth, shall I say? in different quantity or degree.

15. Man is the last and highest manifestation of divine energy, the fullest and most complete expression (or pressing out) of God. To man, therefore, is given dominion over all other manifestations.

16. God is not only the creative cause of every visible form of intelligence and life at its commencement, but each moment throughout its existence He lives within every created thing as the life, the ever renewing, re-creating, upbuilding cause of it. He never is and never can be for a moment separated from His creations. Then how can even a sparrow fall to the ground without His knowledge? And "ye are of more value than many sparrows" (Mt. 10:31).

17. God is. Man exists (from ex, out of, and sistere, to stand forth). Man stands forth out of God.

18. Man is a threefold being, made up of Spirit, soul, and body. Spirit, our innermost, real being, the absolute part of us, the I of us, has never changed, though our thoughts and our circumstances may have changed hundreds of times. This part of us is a standing forth of God into visibility. It is the Father in us. At this central part of his being every person can say, "I and the Father are one" (Jn. 10:30), and speak absolute Truth.

19. Mortal mind--that which Paul calls "the mind of the flesh"--is the consciousness of error.

20. The great whole of as yet unmanifested Good, or God, from whom we are projections or offspring, in whom "we live, and move, and have our being" (Acts 17:28) continually, is to me the Father--our Father; "and all ye are brethren" (Mt. 23:8), because all are manifestations of one and the same Spirit. Jesus, recognizing this, said: "call no man your father, upon the earth: for one is your Father, even he who is in heaven (Mt. 23:9). As soon as we recognize our true relationship to all men, we at once slip out of our narrow, personal loves, our "me and mine," into

the universal love that takes in all the world, joyfully exclaiming: "Who is my mother? and who are my brethren?

And he stretched forth his hand toward his disciples, and said, Behold, my mother and my brethren" (Mt. 12:48).

21. Many have thought of God as a personal being. The statement that God is Principle chills them, and in terror they cry out, "They have taken away my Lord, and I know not where they have laid him" (Jn. 20:13).

22. Broader and more learned minds are always cramped by the thought of God as a person, for personality limits to place and time.

23. God is the name we give to that unchangeable, inexorable principle at the source of all existence. To the individual consciousness God takes on personality, but as the creative underlying cause of all things, He is principle, impersonal; as expressed in each individual, He becomes personal to that one--a personal, loving, all-forgiving Father-Mother. All that we can ever need or desire is the infinite Father-Principle, the great reservoir of unexpressed good. There is no limit to the Source of our being, nor to His willingness to manifest more of Himself through us, when we are willing to do his will.

24. Hitherto we have turned our heart and efforts toward the external for fulfillment of our desires and for satisfaction, and we have been grievously disappointed. The hunger of everyone for satisfaction is only the cry of the homesick child for its Father-Mother God. It is only the Spirit's desire in us to come forth into our consciousness as more and more perfection, until we shall have become fully

conscious of our oneness with All-perfection. Man never has been and never can be satisfied with anything less.

25. We all have direct access through the Father in us--the central "I" of our being--to the great whole of life, love, wisdom, power, which is God. What we now want to know is how to receive more from the fountainhead and to make more and more of God (which is but another name for All-Good) manifest in our daily life.

26. There is but one Source of being. This Source is the living fountain of all good, be it life, love, wisdom, power--the Giver of all good gifts. This source and you are connected, every moment of your existence. You have power to draw on this Source for all of good you are, or ever will be, capable of desiring.

46. Oh, if we could only realize that this mighty power to save and to perfect, to deliver and to make alive, lives forever within us, and so cease now and forever looking away to others!

47. There is but one way to obtain this full realization--the way of the Christ. "I am the way, and the truth, and the life" (Jn. 14:6), spoke the Christ through the lips of the Nazarene.

48. Your holding to the words, "Christ is the way," when you are perplexed and confused and can see no way of escape, will invariably open a way of complete deliverance.

Lesson 3

Thinking

1. We learned in the second lesson that the real substance within everything we see is God; that all things are one and the same Spirit in different degrees of manifestation; that all the various forms of life are just the same as one life come forth out of the invisible into visible form; that all the intelligence and all the wisdom in the world are God as wisdom in various degrees of manifestation; that all the love which people feel and express toward others is just a little, so to speak, of God as love come into visibility through the human form.

2. When we say there is but one Mind in the entire universe, and that this Mind is God, some persons, having followed understandingly the first lesson, and recognized God as the one life, one Spirit, one power, pushing Himself out into various degrees of manifestation through people and things, will at once say: "Yes, that is all plain."

3. But someone else will say: "If all the mind there is, is God, then how can I think wrong thoughts, or have any but God thoughts?"

4. The connection between universal Mind and our own individual minds is one of the most difficult things to put into words, but when it once dawns on one, it is easily seen.

5. There is in reality only one Mind (or Spirit, which is life, intelligence, and so forth) in the universe; and yet there is a sense in which we are individuals, or separate, a sense in which we are free wills and not puppets.

6. Man is made up of Spirit, soul, and body. Spirit is the central unchanging "I" of us, the part that since infancy has never changed, and to all eternity never will change. That which some persons call "mortal minds" is the region of the intellect where we do conscious thinking and are free wills. This part of our being is in constant process of changing.

7. In our outspringing from God into the material world, Spirit is inner--one with God; soul is the clothing, as it were, of Spirit; body is the external clothing of the soul. Yet all are in reality one, the composite man--as steam, water, and ice are one, only in different degrees of condensation. In thinking of ourselves, we must not separate Spirit, soul, and body, but rather hold all as one, if we would be strong and powerful. Man originally lived consciously in the spiritual part of himself. He fell by descending in his consciousness to the external or more material part of himself.

8. "Mortal mind," the term so much used and so distracting to many, is the error consciousness, which gathers its information from the outside world through the five senses. It is what Paul calls "the mind of the flesh" in contradistinction to spiritual mind; and he flatly says: "The mind of the flesh [believing what the carnal mind says] is death [sorrow, trouble, sickness]; but the mind of the Spirit [ability to still the carnal mind and let the Spirit speak within us] is life and peace."

9. The Spirit within you is Divine Mind, the real mind. Without it human mind would disappear, just as a shadow disappears when the real thing that casts it is removed.

10. If you find this subject of human mind and universal Mind puzzling to you, do not worry over it. Just drop it for

the time, and as you go on with the lesson, you will find that some day an understanding of it will flash suddenly upon you with perfect clearness.

11. There are today two classes of people, so far as mentality goes, who are seeking deliverance out of sickness, trouble, and unhappiness, by spiritual means. One class requires that every statement made be proved by the most elaborate and logical argument, before it can or will be received. The other class is willing at once to "become as little children" (Mt. 18:3) and just be taught how to take the first step toward pure understanding (or knowledge of Truth as God sees it), and then receives the light by direct revelation from the All-Good. Both are seeking and eventually both will reach the same goal, and neither one should be unduly condemned.

12. If you are one who seeks and expects to get any realizing knowledge of spiritual things through argument or reasoning, no matter how scholarly your attainments or how great you are in worldly wisdom, you are a failure in spiritual understanding. You are attempting an utter impossibility--that of crowding the Infinite into the quart measure of your own intellectual capacity.

13. "The natural man receiveth not the things of the Spirit of God: for they are foolishness unto him; and he cannot know them, because they are spiritually judged" (1 Cor. 2:14). Eventually you will find that you are only beating around on the outside of the "Kingdom of heaven," though in close proximity to it, and you will then become willing to let your intellect take the place of the little child, without which no man can enter in.

14. "Eye hath not seen, nor ear heard, neither have entered into the heart of man, the things which God hath [not will] prepared for them that love him.

15. "But God hath revealed them unto us by his Spirit. . . .
16. "For who among men knoweth the things of a man, save the spirit of the man, which is in him? even so the things of God none knoweth, save the Spirit of God" (1 Cor.2:11).

17. For all those who must wade through months and perhaps years of this purely intellectual or mental process, there are today many books to help, and many teachers of metaphysics who are doing noble and praiseworthy work in piloting these earnest seekers after Truth and satisfaction. To them we cry: "All speed!"

18. But we believe with Paul that "the foolishness of God is wiser than men" (1 Cor. 1:25), and that each man has direct access to all there is in God. We are waiting for the "little Children" who, without question or discussion, are willing at once to accept and try a few plain, simple rules such as Jesus taught the common people, who "heard him gladly"-- rules by which they can find the Christ (or the Divine) within themselves, that through it each man for himself may work out his own salvation from all his troubles.

19. In other words, there is a shortcut to the top of the hill; and while there is a good but long, roundabout road for those who need it, we prefer the less laborious means of attaining the some ends by seeking directly the Spirit of truth promised to dwell in us and to lead us into all Truth. My advice is: If you want to make rapid progress in growth toward spiritual understanding, stop reading many books. They only give someone's opinion about Truth, or a sort of

history of the author's experience in seeking Truth. What you want is revelation of Truth in your own soul, and that will never come through the reading of many books.

20. Seek light from the Spirit of Truth within you. Go alone. Think alone. Seek light alone, and if it does not come at once, do not be discouraged and run off to someone else to get light; for, as we said before, by so doing you get only the opinion of the intellect, and may be then further away from the Truth you are seeking than ever before; for the mortal mind may make false reports.

21. The very Spirit of truth is at your call. "The anointing which ye received of him abideth in you" (1 Jn. 2:27). Seek it. Wait patiently for it to "guide you into the truth" (Jn. 16:13) about all things.

22. "Have this mind in you, which was also in Christ Jesus" (Phil. 2:5). This is the universal Mind, which makes no mistake. Still the intellect for the time being, and let universal Mind speak to you; and when it speaks, though it be but a "still small voice" (1 Kings 19:12), you will know that what it says is Truth.

23. How will you know? You will know just as you know that you are alive. All the argument in the world to convince you against Truth that comes to you through direct revelation will fall flat and harmless at your side. And the Truth that you know, not simply believe, you can use to help others. That which comes forth through your spirit will reach the very innermost spirit of him to whom you speak.

24. What is born from the outside, or intellectual perception, reaches only the intellect of him you would help.

25. The intellect that is servant to the real Mind, and when servant (but not when master) is good, loves to argue; but when its information is based on the evidence of the senses and not on the true thoughts of the Divine Mind, it is very fallible and full of error.

26. Intellect argues. Spirit takes the deep things of God and reveals Truth to man. One may be true; the other always is true. Spirit does not give opinions about Truth; it is Truth, and it reveals itself.

27. Someone has truly said that the merest child who has learned from the depths of his being to say, "Our Father," is infinitely greater than the most intellectual man who has not yet learned it. Paul was a man of gigantic intellect, learned in all the law, a Pharisee of the Pharisees; but after he was spiritually illumined he wrote, "The foolishness of God is wiser than men; and the weakness of God is stronger than men" (1 Cor. 1:25).

28. It does make a great difference in our daily lives what we think about God, about ourselves, about our neighbors. Heretofore, through ignorance of our real selves and of the results of our thinking, we have let our thoughts flow at random. Our minds have been turned toward the external of our being, and nearly all our information has been gotten through our five senses. We have thought wrong because misinformed by these senses, and our troubles and sorrows are the results of our wrong thinking.

29. "But," says someone, "I do not see how my thinking evil or wrong thoughts about God, or about anyone, can make me sick or my husband lose his position."

30. Well, I will not just now try to explain all the steps by which bad results follow false thinking, but I will just ask you to try thinking true, right thoughts awhile, and see what the result will be.

31. Take the thought, "God loves me." Think these words over and over continually for a few days, trying to realize that they are true, and see what the effect will be on your body and circumstances.

32. First, you get a new exhilaration of mind, with a great desire and a sense of power to please God; then a quicker, better circulation of blood, with a sense of pleasant warmth in the body, followed by better digestion. Later, as Truth flows out through your being into your surroundings, everybody will begin to manifest a new love for you without your knowing why; and finally, circumstances will begin to change and fall into harmony with your desires, instead of being adverse to them.

33. Everyone knows how strong thoughts of fear or grief have turned hair white in a few hours; how great fear makes the heart beat so rapidly as to seem about to "jump out of the body," this result not being at all dependent on whether there be any real cause of fear or whether it be a purely imaginary cause. Just so, strong negative thoughts may render the blood acid, causing rheumatism. Bearing mental burdens makes more stooped shoulders than does bearing heavy material loads. Believing that God regards us as "miserable sinners," that He is continually watching us

and our failures with disapproval, bring utter discouragement and a sort of half paralyzed condition of the mind and body, which means failure in all our undertakings.

34. Is it difficult for you to understand why, if God lives in us all the time, He does not keep our thoughts right instead of permitting us through ignorance to drift into wrong thoughts, and so bring trouble on ourselves?

35. Well, we are not automatons. Your child will never learn to walk alone if you always do his walking. Because you recognize that the only way for him to be strong, self-reliant in all things--in other words, to become a man--is to throw him on himself, and let him, through experience, come to a knowledge of things for himself, you are not willing to make a mere puppet of him by taking the steps for him, even though you know that he will fall down many times and give himself severe bumps in his ongoing toward perfect physical manhood.

36. We are in process of growth into the highest spiritual manhood and womanhood. We get many falls and bumps on the way, but only through these, not necessarily by them, can our growth proceed. Father and mother, no matter how strong or deep their love, cannot grow for their children; nor can God, who is omnipotence, at the center of our being, grow spiritually for us without making of us automatons instead of individuals.

37. If you keep your thoughts turned toward the external of yourself, or of others, you will see only the things that are not real, but temporal, and which pass away. All the faults, failures, or lacks in people or circumstances will seem very real to you, and you will be unhappy and sick.

38. If you turn your thoughts away from the external toward the spiritual, and let them dwell on the good in yourself and in others, all the apparent evil will first drop out of your thoughts and then out of your life. Paul understood this when he wrote to the Philippians: "Finally, brethen, whatsoever things are true, whatsoever things are honorable, whatsoever things are just, whatsoever things are pure, whatsoever things are lovely, whatsoever things are of good report; if there be any virtue, and if there be any praise, think on these things" (Phil. 4:8).

39. We all can learn how to turn the conscious mind toward universal Mind, or Spirit, within us. We can, by practice, learn how to make this everyday, topsy-turvy, "mind of the flesh" be still and let the mind that is in God (all-wisdom, all-love) think in us and out through us.

40. Imagine, if you will, a great reservoir, out of which lead innumerable small rivulets or channels. At its farther end each channel opens out into a small fountain. This fountain is not only being continually filled and replenished from the reservoir but is itself a radiating center whence it gives out in all directions that which it receives, so that all who come within its radius are refreshed and blessed.

41. This is our relation with God. Each one of us is a radiating center. Each one, no matter how small or ignorant, is the little fountain at the far end of a channel, the other end of which leads out from all there is in God. This fountain represents the individuality, as separate from the great reservoir--God--and yet as one with Him, and without Him we are nothing.

42. Each of us, no matter how insignificant he may be in the world, may receive from God unlimited good of whatever kind he desires, and radiate it to all about him. But remember, he must radiate if he would receive more. Stagnation is death.

43. Oh, I want the simplest mind to grasp the idea that the very wisdom of God--the love, the life, and the power of God--are ready and waiting with longing impulse to flow out through us in unlimited degree! When it flows in unusual degree through the intellect of a certain person men exclaim, "What a wonderful mind!" When it flows through the hearts of men it is the love that melts all bitterness, envy, selfishness, jealousy, before it; when it flows through their bodies as life, no disease can withstand its onward march.

44. We do not have to beseech God any more than we have to beseech the sun to shine. The sun shines because it is a law of its being to shine, and it cannot help it. No more can God help pouring into us unlimited wisdom, life, power, all good, because to give is a law of His being. Nothing can hinder Him except our own lack of understanding. The sun may shine ever so brightly, but if we have, through willfulness or ignorance, placed ourselves, or have been placed by our progenitors, in the far corner of a damp, dark cellar, we get neither joy nor comfort from its shining; then to us the sun never shines.

45. So we have heretofore known nothing of how to get ourselves out of the cellar of ignorance, doubts, and despair; to our wrong thinking, God has seemed to withhold the life, wisdom, and power we wanted so much, though we sought Him ever so earnestly.

46. The sun does not radiate life and warmth today and darkness and chill tomorrow; it cannot, from the nature of its being. Nor does God radiate love at one time, while at other times, anger, wrath, and displeasure flow from His mind toward us.

47. "Doth the fountain send forth from the same opening sweet water and bitter? can a fig tree, my brethren, yield olives, or a vine figs" (Jas. 3:11).

48. God is All-Good--always good, always love. He never changes, no matter what we do or may have done. He is always trying to pour more of Himself through us into visibility so as to make us grander, larger, fuller, freer individuals.

49. While the child is crying out for its Father-Mother God, the Father-Mother is yearning with infinite tenderness to satisfy the child.

"In the heart of man a cry,

In the heart of God, supply."

RECAPITULATION

50. There is but one Mind in the universe.

51. Human mind, or intellect, makes mistakes because it gathers much information from without.

52. Universal Mind sees and speaks from within, it is all Truth.

53. Our way of thinking makes our happiness or unhappiness, our success or nonsuccess. We can, by effort, change our ways of thinking.

54. God is at all times, regardless of our so-called sins, trying to pour more good into our lives to make them richer and more successful.

Lesson 4

Denials

Then said Jesus unto his disciples, If any man will come after me, let him deny himself, and take up his cross, and follow me--Mt. 16:24.

1. All systems for spiritualizing the mind include denial. Every religion in all the ages had some sort of denial as one of its foundations. We all know how the Puritans believed that the more rigidly they denied themselves comfort the better they pleased God. So far has this idea taken possession of the human mind during some ages that devout souls have even tortured their bodies in various ways, believing that they were thus making themselves more spiritual, or at least were in some way placating an angry God. Even today many interpret the above-quoted saying of Jesus as meaning: If any man wants to please God he must give up about all the enjoyment and comfort he has, all things he likes and wants, and must take up the heavy cross of constantly doing the things that are repugnant to him in his daily life. This is why many young people say, "When I am old I will be a Christian, but not now, for I want to enjoy life awhile first."

2. There could, I am sure, be nothing further from the meaning of the Nazarene than the foregoing interpretation.

In our ignorance of the nature of God, our Father, and of our relationship to Him, we have believed that all our enjoyment came from external sources, usually from gaining possession of something we did not have. The poor see enjoyment only in possessing abundance of money. The rich, who are satiated with life's so-called pleasures until their lives have become like a person with an over-loaded stomach, compelled to sit constantly at a well-spread table, are often the most bitter in the complaint that life holds no happiness for them. The sick one believes that, were he well, he would be perfectly happy. The healthy but hard working person feels the need of some days of rest and recreation, that the monotony of his life may be broken.

3. So ever the mind has been turned to some external change of condition or circumstance in pursuit of satisfaction and enjoyment. In after years, when men have tried all, getting first this thing and then that, which they thought would yield them happiness, and have been grievously disappointed, in a kind of desperation they turn to God and try to find some sort of comfort in believing that sometime, somewhere, they will get what they want and be happy. Thenceforth their lives are patient and submissive, but they are destitute of any real joy.

4. This same Nazarene, to whom we always return because to us He is the best-known teacher and demonstrator of Truth, spent nearly three years teaching the people--the common everyday people like you and me, who wanted, just as we do, food and rent and clothing, money, friends, and love--to love their enemies and to do good to those who persecuted them, to resist not evil in any way, but to give double to anyone who tried to get what belonged to them; to cease from all anxiety regarding the things they needed because "your heavenly Father knoweth that ye

have need of all these things" (Mt. 6:32). And then talking one day He said, "These things have I spoken unto you, that my joy might remain in you, and that your joy might be full" (Jn. 15:11). And He continued, "Whatsoever ye shall ask of the Father in my name, he may give it to you" (Jn. 15:16). "Ask and ye shall receive, that your joy may be full. . . I say not unto you, that I will pray the Father for you: for the Father himself loveth you" (Jn. 16:24-26). We have further learned that God is the total of all the good in the universe and that there is in the mind which is God a perpetual desire to pour more of Himself--the substance of all good things--through us into visibility, or into our lives.

5. Surely all these things do not make it look as though, when Jesus said that the way to be like him and to possess a like power was to deny oneself, He meant that we are to go without the enjoyable comforts of life or in any way deprive or torture ourselves.

6. In these lessons we have seen that, besides the real innermost self of each of us--the self that is the divine self because it is an expression or pressing out of God into visibility and is always one with the Father--there is a human self, a carnal mind, which reports lies from the external world and is not to be relied upon fully; this is the self of which Jesus spoke when He said, "let him deny himself." This intellectual man, carnal mind, or whatever you choose to call him, is envious and jealous and fretful and sick because he is selfish. The human self seeks its own gratification at the expense, if need be, of someone else.

7. Your real self is never sick, never afraid, never selfish. It is the part of you that "seeketh not her own, is not easily provoked, thinketh no evil" (1 Cor. 13:5). It is always

seeking to give to others, while the human self is always seeking its own. Heretofore we have lived more in the human region. We have believed all that the carnal mind has told us, and the consequence is that we have been overwhelmed with all kinds of privation and suffering.

8. Some people who, during the last few years, have been making a special study of the mind find it a fact that certain wrong or false beliefs held by us are really the cause of all sorts of trouble--physical, moral, and financial. They have learned that wrong (or, as they call them, error) beliefs arise only in the human mind; they have learned and actually proved that we can, by a persistent effort of the will, change the beliefs, and by this means alone entirely change our troublesome circumstances and bodily conditions.

9. One of the methods that they have found will work every time in getting rid of troublesome conditions (which are all the result of erroneous thinking and feeling) is to deny them in toto: First, to deny that any such things have, or could have, power to make us unhappy; second, to deny that these things do in reality exist at all.

10. The word deny has two definitions, according to Webster. To deny, in one sense, is to withhold from, as to deny bread to the hungry. To deny, in another sense (and we believe it was in this latter way that Jesus used it), is to declare to be not true, to repudiate as utterly false. To deny oneself, then, is not to withhold comfort or happiness from the external man, much less to inflict torture upon him, but it is to deny the claims of error consciousness, to declare these claims to be untrue.

11. If you have done any piece of work incorrectly, the very first step toward getting it right is to undo the wrong, and begin again from that point. We have believed wrong about God and about ourselves. We have believed that God was angry with us and that we were sinners who ought to be afraid of Him. We have believed that sickness and poverty and other troubles are evil things put here by this same God to torture us in some way into serving Him and loving Him. We have believed that we have pleased God best when we became so absolutely subdued by our troubles as to be patiently submissive to them all, not even trying to rise out of them or to overcome them. All this is false, entirely false! And the first step toward freeing ourselves from our troubles is to get rid of our erroneous beliefs about God and about ourselves.

12. "But," objects one, "if a thing is not true and I have believed a lie about it, I do not see just how my believing wrong about it could affect my bodily health or my circumstances."

13. A child can be so afraid of an imaginary bugaboo under the bed as to have convulsions. Should you, today, receive a telegraphic message that your husband, wife, or child, who is absent from you, had been suddenly killed, your suffering, mental and physical, and perhaps extending even to your external and financial affairs, would be just as great as though the report really were true; and yet it might be entirely false. Exactly so have these messages of bugaboos behind the doors, bugaboos of divine wrath and of our own weakness, come to us through the senses until we are overcome by our fears of them.

14. Now, let us arouse ourselves. Denial is the first practical step toward wiping out of our minds the mistaken

beliefs of a lifetime--the beliefs that have made such sad
havoc of our lives. By denial we mean declaring not to be
true a thing that seems true. Negative appearances are
directly opposed to the teachings of Truth. Jesus said,
"Judge not according to appearance, but judge righteous
[right] judgment" (Jn. 7:24).

15. Suppose you had always been taught that the sun really
moved or revolved around the earth, and someone should
now persuade you that the opposite is the truth. You would
see at once that such might be the case, and yet as often as
you saw the sun rise, the old impression, made on your
mind by the wrong belief of years, would come up and
seem almost too real to be disputed. The only way by
which you could cleanse your mind of the impression and
make the untrue seem unreal, would be by repeatedly
denying the old beliefs, saying over and over to yourself as
often as the subject came up in your mind: "This is not true.
The sun does not move; it stands still, and the earth
moves." Eventually the sun would only seem to move.

16. The appearances are that our bodies and our
circumstances control our thoughts, but the opposite is true.
Our thoughts control our bodies and our circumstances.
17. If you repeatedly deny a false or unhappy condition, it
loses its power to make you unhappy.

18. What everyone desires is to have only the good
manifested in his life and surroundings--to have his life full
of love; to have perfect health; to know all things; to have
great power and much joy; and this is just exactly what
God wants us to have. All love is God in manifestation, as
we have learned in a previous lesson. All wisdom is God.
All life and health are God. All joy (because all good) and
all power are God. All good of whatever kind is God come

forth into visibility through people or some other visible form. When we crave more of any good thing, we are in reality craving more of God to come forth into our lives so that we can realize it by our senses. Having more of God does not take out of our lives the good things--it only puts more of them in. In the mind that is God there is always the desire to give more, for the divine plan is forever to get more good into visibility.

19. Intellectually we may see the fact of our own God-being, which never changes. What we need is to realize our oneness with the Father at all times. In order to realize it we deny ourselves and others the appearances that seem contrary to this--deny them as realities; we declare that they are not true.

20. There are four common error thoughts to which nearly everyone grants great power. Persons who have grown out of sickness and trouble through prayer have found it good to deny these thoughts, in order to cleanse the mind of the direful effects of believing them. They can be denied like this.

21. First: There is no evil.

22. There is but one power in the universe, and that is God--good. God is good, and God is omnipresent. Apparent evils are not entities or things of themselves. They are simply apparent absence of the good, just as darkness is an absence of light. But God, or good, is omnipresent, so the apparent absence of good (evil) is unreal. It is only an appearance of evil, just as the moving sun was an appearance. You need not wait to discuss this matter of evil or to understand fully all about why you deny it, but begin to practice the denials in an unprejudiced way, and see how

marvelously they will, after a while, deliver you from some of the so-called evils of your daily life.

23. Second: There is no absence of life, substance, or intelligence anywhere.

24. We have seen that the real is the spiritual. "The things which are seen are temporal; but the things which are not seen are eternal" (2 Cor. 4:18). By using this denial you will soon break your bondage to matter and to material conditions. You will know that you are free.

25. Third: Pain, sickness, poverty, old age, and death cannot master me, for they are not real.

26. Fourth: There is nothing in all the universe for me to fear, for greater is He that is within me than he that is in the world.

27. God says, "I will contend with him that contendeth with thee" (Is. 49:25). He says it to every living child of His, and every person is His child.

28. Repeat these four denials silently several times a day, not with a strained anxiety to get something out of them, but trying calmly to realize the meaning of the words spoken:

29. There is no evil.

30. There is no absence of life, substance, or intelligence anywhere.

31. Pain, sickness, poverty, old age, and death cannot master me, for they are not real.

32. There is nothing in all the universe for me to fear, for greater is He that is within me than he that is in the world.

33. Almost hourly little vexations and fears come up in your life. Meet each one with a denial. Calmly and cooly say within yourself, "That's nothing at all. It cannot harm or disturb me or make me unhappy." Do not fight it vigorously, but let your denial be the denial of any thought of its superiority over you, as you would deny the power of ants on their little hill to disturb you. If you are angry, stand still, and silently deny it. Say that you are not angry; that you are love made manifest, and cannot be angry and the anger will leave you.

34. If someone shows you ill will, silently deny his power to hurt you or to make you unhappy. Should you find yourself feeling jealous or envious toward anyone, instantly turn the heel of denial on the hydraheaded monsters. Declare that you are not jealous or envious; that you are an expression of perfect love (an expression which is God pressed out into visibility) and cannot feel negation. There is really no reason for jealousy or envy, for all persons are one and the same spirit. "And there are diversities of operations [or manifestations], but it is the same God which worketh all in all" (1 Cor. 12:6), says Paul. How can you be envious of a part of yourself that seems to you more comely?

35. Shall the foot be envious of the hand, or the ear of the eye? Are not the seemingly feeble members of the body as important to the perfection of the whole as the others? Do you seem to be less, or to have less, than some others? Remember that all envy and all jealousy are in the error consciousness and that in reality you, however

insignificant, are an absolute necessity to God in order to make the perfect whole.

36. If you find yourself dreading to meet anyone, or afraid to step out and do what you want or ought to do, immediately begin to say, "It is not true; I am not afraid; I am perfect love, and can know no fear. No one, nothing in all the universe, can hurt me." You will find after a little that all the fear has disappeared, all trepidation has gone.

37. Denial brings freedom from bondage, and happiness comes when we effectually deny the power of anything to touch or trouble us.

38. Have you been living in negation for years, denying your ability to succeed, denying your health, denying your Godhood, denying your power to accomplish anything, by feeling yourself a child of the Devil or of weakness? If so, this constant negation has paralyzed you and weakened your power.

39. When, in the next lesson, you learn something about affirmations, the opposite of denials, you will know how to lift yourself out of the realm of failure into that of success.

40. All your happiness, all your health and power, come from God. They flow in an unbroken stream from the fountainhead into the very center of your being and radiate from center to circumference. When you acknowledge this constantly and deny that outside things can hinder your happiness or health or power, it helps you to realize health and power and happiness.

41. No person or thing in the universe, no chain of circumstances, can by any possibility interpose itself

between you and all joy--all good. You may think that
something stands between you and your heart's desire, and
so live with that desire unfulfilled; but it is not true. This
"think" is the bugaboo under the bed that has no reality.
Deny it, deny it, and you will find yourself free, and you
will realize that this seeming was all false. Then you will
see the good flowing into you, and you will see clearly that
nothing can stand between you and your own.

42. Denials may be spoken silently or audibly, but not in a
manner to call forth antagonism and discussion.

43. To some, all this sort of mechanical working will seem
a strange way of entering into a more spiritual life. There
are those who easily and naturally glide out of the old
material life into a deeper spiritual one without any
external help; but there are thousands of others who are
seeking primarily the loaves and fishes of bodily health and
financial success, but who really are seeking a higher way
of life, who must needs take the very first steps. For such,
the practicing of these mechanical steps in a wholehearted
way, without prejudice, is doing the very best thing
possible toward attaining purity of heart and life, toward
growth in divine knowledge and fullness of joy in all things
undertaken.

Lesson 5

Affirmations

Thou shalt make thy prayer unto him, and he will hear thee;
And thou shalt pay thy vows, Thou shalt also decree a
thing, and it shall be established unto thee; and light
shall shine upon thy ways--Job 22:27,28.

1. Most persons, when they first consciously set out to gain
a fuller, higher knowledge of spiritual things, do so because
of dissatisfaction--or perhaps unsatisfaction would be the
better word--with their present conditions of life. Inherent
in the human mind is the thought that somewhere,
somehow, it ought to be able to bring to itself that which it
desires and which would satisfy. This thought is but the
foreshadowing of that which really is.

2.

Our wishes, it is said, do measure just
Our capabilities, Who with his might
Aspires unto the mountain's upper height,
Holds in that aspiration a great trust
To be filled, a warrant that he must
Not disregard, a strength to reach the height
To which his hopes have taken flight.
--Author Unknown

3. The hunger that we feel is but the prompting of the
Divine within us, which longs with an infinite longing to
fill us. It is but one side of the law of demand and supply,
the other side of which is unchangeable, unfailing, the
promise: "All things whatsoever ye pray and ask for,
believe that ye receive them, and ye shall have them" (Mk.

11:24). The supply is always equal to the demand, but there must first be a demand before supply is of use.

4. There is, attainable by us, a place where we can see that our doing can cease, because we realize that Spirit is the fulfillment of all our desires. We simply get still and know that all things whatsoever we desire are ours already; and this knowing it, or recognizing it, has power to bring the invisible God (or good)--the innermost substance of all things--forth into just the visible form of good that we want.

5. But in order to attain this place of power, we must take the preliminary steps, faithfully, earnestly, trustingly, though these steps at first glance seem to us useless and as empty as do the ceremonial forms and religious observance of the ritualistic churchman.

6. To affirm anything is to assert positively that it is so, even in the face of all contrary evidence. We may not be able to see how, by our simply affirming a thing to be true, a thing that to all human reasoning or sight does not seem to be true at all, we can bring this thing to pass; but we can compel ourselves to cease all futile quibbling and go to work to prove the rule, each one in his own life.

7. The beautiful Presence all about us and within us is the substance of every good that we can possibly desire--aye, infinitely more than we are capable of desiring; for "Eye hath not seen, nor ear heard, neither have entered into the heart of man, the things which God hath prepared for them that love him" (1 Cor. 2:9 A.V.).

8. In some way, which is not easy to put into words--for spiritual words cannot always be compassed in words, and

yet they are none the less infallible, immutable laws that work with precision and certainty--there is power in our word of faith to bring all things right into our everyday life.

9. We speak the word, we confidently affirm, but we have nothing to do with the "establishing" of the word, or bringing it to pass. "Thou shalt also decree a thing, and it shall be established unto thee" (Job 22:28). So if we decree or affirm unwaveringly, steadfastly, we hold God by His own unalterable laws to do the establishing or fulfilling.

10. They who have carefully studied spiritual laws find that, besides denying the reality and power of apparent evil, which denying frees them from it, they also can bring any desired good into their lives by persistently affirming it is there already. In the first instructions given to students, the denials and affirmations take a large place. Later on, their own personal experiences and inward guidance lead them to an understanding of divine law that makes it easy for them to follow simple rules which at first seemed difficult.

11. The saying over and over of any denial or affirmation is a necessary training of the mind that has lived so long in error and false belief that it needs this constant repetition of Truth to unclothe it and to clothe it anew.

12. As it is with the denials, so with the affirmations. There are four or five sweeping affirmations of Truth that cover a multitude of lesser ones, and which do marvelous work in bringing good to ourselves and to others.

13. First: God is life, love, intelligence, substance, omnipotence, omniscience, omnipresence.

14. These ideas you learned in the second lesson--
"Statement of Being." As you repeat the affirmation, please
remember that every particle of life, love, intelligence,
power, or of real substance in the universe, is simply a
certain degree, or, so to speak, a quantity of God made
manifest or visible through a form. Try to think what it
means when you say that God is omnipresent, omnipotent,
omniscient.

15. God is omnipresence (everywhere present), and God is
good. Then why fear evil? He is omnipotent (all powerful).
Then what other power can prevail?

16. Since God is omnipotence and omnipresence, put aside
forever your traditional teaching of an adverse power, evil
(Devil), that may at any moment thwart the plans of God
and bring harm to you.

17. Do not disturb yourself about appearance of evil all
about you; but in the very presence of what seems evil
stand true and unwavering in affirming that God, the good
is omnipresent. By so doing, you will see the seeming evil
melt away as the darkness before the light or as the dew
before the morning sun, and good come to take its place.

18. Second: I am a child or manifestation of God, and every
moment His life, love, wisdom, power flow into and
through me. I am one with God, and am governed by His
law.

19. Remember while repeating this affirmation that
nothing--no circumstance, no person or set of persons--can
by any possibility interpose between you and the Source of
your life, wisdom, or power. It is all "hid with Christ [the

innermost Christ or Spirit of your being] in God" (Col. 3:3). Nothing but your own ignorance of how to receive, or your willfulness, can hinder your having unlimited supply.

20. No matter how sick or weak or inefficient you seem to be, take your eyes and thoughts right off the seeming, and turn them within to the central fountain there, and say calmly, quietly, but with steadfast assurance: "This appearance of weakness is false; God, manifest as life, wisdom, and power is now flowing into my entire being and out through me to the external." You will see a marvelous change wrought in yourself by the realization that this spoken word will bring to you.

21. You do not change God's attitude toward you one iota by either importuning or affirming. You only change your attitude toward Him. By thus affirming, you put yourself in harmony with divine law, which is always working toward your good and never toward your harm or punishment.

22. Third: I am Spirit, perfect, holy, harmonious. Nothing can hurt me or make me sick or afraid, for Spirit is God, and God cannot be sick or hurt or afraid. I manifest my real self through this body now.

23. Fourth: God works in me to will and to do whatsoever He wishes me to do, and He cannot fail.

24. Our affirming His mind working both to will and to do, makes us will only the good; and He, the very Father in us, does the works, hence there can be no failure. Whatsoever we fully commit to the Father to do, and affirm it is done, we shall see accomplished. These, then, are the four comprehensive affirmations.

25. First: God is life, love, intelligence, substance, omnipotence, omniscience, omnipresence.

26. Second: I am a child or manifestation of God, and every moment His life, love, wisdom, power flow into and through me. I am one with God, and am governed by His law.

27. Third: I am Spirit, perfect, holy, harmonious. Nothing can hurt me or make me sick or afraid, for Spirit is God, and God cannot be sick or hurt or afraid. I manifest my real self through this body now.

28. Fourth: God works with me to will and to do whatsoever He wishes me to do, and He cannot fail.

29. Commit these affirmations to memory, so that you can repeat them in the silence of your own mind in any place and at any time. Strangely, they will act to deliver you out of the greatest external distresses, places where no human help avails. It is as though the moment you assert emphatically your oneness with God the Father, there is instantly set into motion all the power of omnipotent love to rush to your rescue. And when it has undertaken to work for you, you can cease from external ways and means, and boldly claim: "It is done; I have the desires of my heart."
    "Thou openest thy hand,
  And satisfiest the desire of every living thing"
  .(Ps. 145:16).

30. In reality God is forever in process of movement within us, that He may manifest Himself (all-Good) more fully through us. Our affirming, backed by faith, is the link that connects our conscious human need with His power and supply.

31. They who have claimed their birthright by thus calmly affirming their oneness with God know how free they can be from human planning and effort, after they have called into operation this marvelous power of affirmation. This power has healed the sick, brought joy in place of mourning, literally opened prison doors and bidden the prisoner go free, without the claimants calling for human assistance.

32. Understand, it is not necessarily the using of just this form of words that has availed in each individual case. It is the denying of apparent evil, and, in spite of all contrary evidence, the affirming of good to be all there is, affirming oneness with God's omnipotent power to accomplish, even when there is no visible sign of His being present, that has wrought the deliverance. In one case within my knowledge, just simply claiming, "God is your defense and deliverance," for a man who had for five years been an exile from home and country (through a series of deceptions and machinations that for depth and subtlety were unparalled) opened all the doors wide and restored the man to his family within a month, without any further human effort on the part of himself or his friends, and this after five years of the most strenuous human efforts of lawyers had failed utterly to bring the truth to light or to release the prisoner.

33. Some minds are so constituted that they get better results from repeated use of denials; others, from using denials less and affirmations more.

34. No definite rules can be laid down as to which will work most effectually in each individual case to eradicate apparent evil and bring the good into manifestation, but some little hint that may be helpful can be given.

35. Denials have an erasive or dissolving tendency. Affirmations build up, and give strength and courage and power. Persons who remember vividly, and are inclined to dwell in their thoughts on the pains, sorrows, and troubles of the past or present, need to deny a great deal; for denials cleanse the mind and blot out the memory of all seeming evil and unhappiness, so they become a far away dream. Again, denials are particularly useful to those who are hard and intolerant, or aggressively sinful; to those who, as a result of success have become overconfident, thinking the human is sufficient in itself for all things; to the selfish, and to any who do not scruple to harm others.

36. Affirmations should be used by the timid and by those who have a feeling of their own inefficiency; those who stand in fear of other minds; those who "give in" easily; those who are subject to anxiety or doubt, and those who are in positions of responsibility. Persons who are in any way negative or passive need to use affirmations more; the ones who are self-confident or unforgiving, need denials more.

37. Deny the appearance of evil; affirm good. Deny weakness; affirm strength. Deny undesirable conditions, and affirm the good you desire. This is what Jesus meant when He said, "All things whatsoever ye pray and ask for, believe [or claim and affirm] that ye have received them, and ye shall have them" (Mk. 11:24). This is what is meant by the promise: "Every place that the sole of your foot shall tread upon [or that you stand squarely or firmly upon], to you have I given it" (Josh. 1:3).

38. Practice these denials and affirmations silently in the street, in the car, when you are wakeful during the night, anywhere, everywhere, and they will give you a new, and,

to you, a strange, mastery over external things and over yourself. If there comes a moment when you are in doubt as to what to do, stand still and affirm, "God in me is infinite wisdom; I know just what to do." "For I will give you a mouth and wisdom, which all your adversaries shall not be able to withstand or to gainsay" (Lk. 21:15). Do not get flustered or anxious, but depend fully and trustingly on your principle, and you will be surprised at the sudden inspiration that will come to you as the mode of procedure.

39. So always this principle will work in the solution of all life's problems--I care not what the form of detail is--to free us, God's children, from all undesirable conditions, and to bring good into our lives, if we will take up the simple rules and use them faithfully, until they lead us into such realization of our Godhood that we need no longer consciously depend on them.

Lesson 6

Faith

"Verily I say unto you, Whosoever shall say unto this mountain, Be thou taken up and cast into the sea; and shall not doubt in his heart, but shall believe that what he saith cometh to pass; he shall have it." --Mk. 11:23
"Science was faith once."--Lowell

1. The word faith is one that has generally been thought to denote a simple form of belief based mostly on ignorance and superstition. It is a word that has drawn forth something akin to scorn from so-called "thinking people"-- the people who have believed that intellectual attainment is the highest form of knowledge to be reached. "Blind faith"

they have disdainfully chosen to call it--fit only for
ministers, women, and children, but not a practical thing on
which to establish the everyday business affairs of life.

2. Some have prided themselves on having outgrown the
swaddling clothes of this blind, unreasoning faith, and
having grown to the point, as they say, where they have
faith only in that which can be seen or intellectually
explained.

3. The writer of The Epistle to the Hebrews, obviously a
most intellectual man, and a learned theologian, before
writing at length on the nature of faith and the marvelous
results attending it, tried to put into a few words a
condensed definition of faith:

4. "Faith is the substance of things hoped for, the evidence
of things not seen" (Heb. 11:1 A.V.).

5. In other words, faith takes right hold of the substance of
the things desired, and brings into the world of evidence
the things that before were not seen. Further speaking of
faith, the writer said, "Things which are seen were not
made of things which do appear" (Heb. 11:3 A.V.); that is,
things that are seen are not made out of visible things, but
out of the invisible. In some way, then, we understand that
whatever we want is in this surrounding invisible
substance, and faith is the power that can bring it out into
actuality to us.

6. After having cited innumerable instances of marvelous
things brought to pass in the lives of men, not by their work
or efforts, but by faith, the Epistle says,

7. "And what shall I more say? for the time will fail me to tell of Gideon, Barak, Samson, Jephthah; of David and Samuel and the prophets: who through faith subdued kingdoms, wrought righteousness, obtained promises, stopped the mouths of lions, quenched the power of fire, escaped the edge of the sword, from weakness were made strong, waxed mighty in war, turned to flight armies of aliens. Women received their dead by a resurrection (Heb. 11:32-35).

8. Do you want any more power or any greater thing than is here mentioned--power to subdue kingdoms, to stop the mouths of lions, quench fire, turn to flight whole armies, raise the dead to life again? Even if your desires exceed this, you need not despair or hesitate to claim their fulfillment, for One greater than you, One who knew whereof He spoke, said: "All things are possible to him that believeth" (Mk. 9:23).

9. Until very recently, whenever anyone has spoken of faith as the one power that can move mountains, we have always felt a sort of hopeless discouragement. While we have believed that God holds all good things in His hand, and is willing to be prevailed upon to dole them out according to our faith, yet how could we, even by straining every nerve of our being toward faith, be sure that we had sufficient to please Him? For does it not say, "Without faith it is impossible to be well-pleasing unto him" (Heb. 11:6)?

10. From the moment we began to ask, we began to question our ability to reach God's standard of faith on which hung our fate. We also began to question whether, after all, there is any such power in faith to prevail with the Giver of "every good gift" so as to draw out of Him something that He had never let us have before.

11. Viewing faith in this light, there is not much wonder that logical minds have looked on it as a sort of will-o'-the-wisp, good enough for women and children to hang their hopes on, but not a thing from which any real, definite results could ever be obtained--not a thing that the business world could rest upon.

12. There is a blind faith, to be sure. (someone has truthfully said that blind faith is better than none at all; for, if held to, it will get its eyes open after a time.) But there is also an understanding faith. Blind faith is an instinctive trust in a power higher than ourselves. Understanding faith is based on immutable principle.

13. Faith does not depend on physical facts, or on the evidence of the senses, because it is born of intuition, or the Spirit of truth ever living at the center of our being. Its action is infinitely higher than that of intellectual conclusions; it is founded on Truth.

14. Intuition is the open end, within one's own being, of the invisible channel ever connecting each individual with God. Faith is, as it were, a ray of light shot out from the central sun--God--one end of which rays comes into your being and mine through the open door of intuition. With our consciousness we perceive the ray of light, and though intellect cannot grasp it, or give the why or wherefore thereof, yet we instinctively feel that the other end of the ray opens out into all there is of God (good). This is "blind" faith. It is based on Truth, but a Truth of which everyone is not at the time conscious. Even this kind of faith will, if persisted in, bring results.

15. What is understanding faith? There are some things that God has so indissolubly joined together that it is impossible

for even Him to put them asunder. They are bound together by fixed, immutable laws; if we have one of them, we must have the other.

16. This is illustrated by the laws of geometry

For instance, the sum of the angles of a triangle is equal to two right angles. No matter how large or small the triangle, no matter whether it is made on the mountaintop or leagues under the sea, if we are asked the sum of its angles we can unhesitatingly answer, without waiting an instant to count or reckon this particular triangle, that it is just two right angles. This is absolutely certain. It is certain, even before the triangle is drawn by visible lines; we can know it beforehand, because it is based on unchangeable laws, on the truth or reality of the thing. It was true just as much before anyone recognized it as it is today. Our knowing it or not knowing it does not change the truth. Only in proportion as we come to know it as an eternal truth can we be benefited by it.

17. It is also a simple truth that one plus one equals two; it is an eternal truth. You cannot put one and one together without two resulting. You may believe it or not; that does not alter the truth. But unless you do put the one and one together you do not produce the two, for each is eternally dependent on the other.

18. The mental and spiritual world or realms are governed by laws that are just as real and unfailing as the laws that govern the natural world. Certain conditions of mind are so connected with certain results that the two are inseparable. If we have the one, we must have the other, as surely as the night follows the day--not because we believe some wise person's testimony that such is the case, not even because

the voice of intuition tells us that it is so, but because the whole matter is based on laws that can neither fail nor be broken.

19. When we know something of these laws, we can know positively beforehand just what results will follow certain mental states.

20. God, the one creative cause of all things, is Spirit, and visible to spiritual consciousness, as we have learned. God is the sum total of all good. There is no good that you can desire in your life which, at its center, is not God. God is the substance of all things--the real thing within every visible form of good.

21. God, the invisible substance out of which all visible things are formed, is all around us waiting to come forth into manifestation.

22. This good substance all about us is unlimited, and is itself the supply of every demand that can be made; of every need that exists in the visible or natural world.

23. One of the unerring truths in the universe (by "universe" I mean the spiritual and natural worlds combined) is that there is already provided a lavish abundance for every human want. In other words, the supply of every good always awaits the demand. Another truth is that the demand must be made before the supply can come forth to fill it. To recognize these two statements of Truth and to affirm them are the whole secret of understanding faith--faith based on principle.

24. Let us square this by the definition of faith, given earlier in the lesson: "Faith is the substance of things hoped

for, the evidence of things not seen" (Heb11:1). Faith takes hold of the substance of the thing hoped for, and brings into evidence, or visibility, the things not seen.

25. What are usually called the promises of God are certain eternal, unchangeable truths that are true whether they are found in the Bible or in the almanac. They are unvarying statements of truth that cannot be altered. A promise, according to Webster, is something sent beforehand to indicate that something unseen is at hand. It is a declaration that gives the person to whom it is made the right to expect and claim the performance of the act.

26. The Nazarene recognized the unchangeable truth that, in the unseen, the supply of every want awaits demand. When He said, "Ask, and ye shall receive" (Jn. 16:24), He was simply stating an unalterable truth. He knew that the instant we ask or desire (for asking is desire expressed) we touch a secret spring which starts on its way toward us the good we want. He knew that there need not be any coaxing or pleading about it; that our asking is simply our complying with an unfailing law which is bound to work; there is no escape from it. Asking and receiving are the two ends of the same thing. There is a very close connection between them.

27. Asking springs from desire to possess some good. What is desire? Desire in the heart is always God tapping at the door of your consciousness with His infinite supply--a supply that is forever useless unless there be demand for it. "Before they call, I will answer" (Is. 65:24). Before ever you are conscious of any lack, of any desire for more happiness, for fullness of joy, the great Father-Mother heart has desired them for you. It is He in you desiring them that you feel, and think it is only yourself (separate from Him)

desiring them. With God the desire to give, and giving, are one and the same thing. Someone has said, "Desire for anything is the thing itself in incipiency"; that is, the thing you desire is not only for you, but has already been started toward you out of the heart of God; and it is the first approach of the thing itself striking you that makes you desire it, or even think of it at all.

28. The only way God has of letting us know of His infinite supply and His desire to make it ours is for Him to push gently on the divine spark living within each one of us. He wants you to be a strong, self-efficient man or woman, to have more power and dominion over all before you; so He quietly and silently pushes a little more of Himself, His desire, into the center of your being. He enlarges, so to speak, your real self, and at once you become conscious of new desire to be bigger, grander, stronger. If He had not pushed at the center of your being first, you would never have thought of new desires, but would have remained perfectly content as you were.

29. You think that you want better health, more love, a brighter, more cheerful home all your very own; in short, you want less evil (or no evil) and more good in your life. This is only God pushing at the inner door of your being, as if He were saying: "My child, let Me in; I want to give you all good, that you may be more comfortable and happy." "Behold, my servants shall eat. . .behold, my servants shall drink. . .behold my servants shall rejoice. . .behold, my servants shall sing for joy of heart. . .And they shall build houses, and inhabit them" (Is. 65:13, 14, 21).

30. Remember this: Desire in the heart for anything is God's sure promise sent beforehand to indicate that it is

yours already in the limitless realm of supply, and whatever you want you can have for the taking.

31. Taking is simply recognizing the law of supply and demand (even if you cannot see a sign of the supply any more than Elijah did when he had affirmed for rain, and not a cloud even so big as a man's hand was for a long time to be seen). Affirm your possession of the good that you desire; have faith in it, because you are working with divine law and cannot fail; do not be argued off your basic principle by anyone; and sooner will the heavens fall than that you fail to get that which you desire.

32. "All things whatsoever ye pray and ask for, believe that ye receive them, and ye shall have them" (Mk. 11:24).

33. Knowing the law of abundant supply, and the truth that supply always precedes the demand, demand simply being the call that brings the supply into sight; knowing that all desire in the heart for any good is really God's desire in us and for us, how shall we obtain the fulfillment of our every desire, and that right speedily?

34. "Delight thyself also in Jehovah; And he will give thee the desires of thy heart" (Ps. 37:4). Take right hold of God with an unwavering faith. Begin and continue to rejoice, and thank Him that you have (not will have) the desires of your heart, never losing sight of the fact that the desire is the thing itself in incipiency. If the good were not already yours in the invisible realm of supply, you could not, by any possibility, desire it.

35. Someone asks: "Suppose I desire my neighbor's wife, or his property; is that desire born of God? And can I see it fulfilled by affirming that it is mine?"

36. You do not and cannot, by any possibility, desire that which belongs to another. You do not desire your neighbor's wife. You desire the love that seems to you to be represented by your neighbor's wife. You desire something to fill your heart's craving for love. Affirm that there is for you a rightful and an overflowing supply, and claim its manifestation. It will surely come, and your so-called desire to possess your neighbor's wife will suddenly disappear.

37. So you do not in reality desire anything that belongs to your neighbor. You want the equivalent of that for which his possessions stand. You want your own. There is today an unlimited supply of all good provided in the unseen for every human being. No man must needs have less that another may have more. Your very own awaits you. Your understanding faith, or trust, is the power that will bring it to you.

38. Emerson said that the man who knows the law "is sure that his welfare is dear to the heart of being. . .He believes that he cannot escape from his good."

39. Knowing divine law and obeying it, we can forever rest from all anxiety, all fear, for "Thou openest thy hand, And satisfiest the desire of every living thing" (Ps. 145:16).

Lesson 7

Personality and Individuality

1. One of the greatest beauties of the Sermon on the Mount
is the childlike simplicity of its language. Every child,
every grown person, be he ever so uneducated, if he can
read at all can understand it. Not a word in it requires the
use of a dictionary; not a sentence in it that does not tell the
way so plainly that "the wayfaring men, yea, fools, shall
not err therein" (Is. 35:8). And yet the Nazarene was the
fullest, most complete manifestation of the one Mind that
has ever lived; that is to say, more of the wisdom that is
God came forth through Him into visibility than through
anyone else who has ever lived. The more any person
manifests the true wisdom, which is God, the more simple
are his ways of thinking and acting; the more simple are the
words through which he expresses his ideas. The greater
the truth to be expressed, the more simple can it (and
should it) be clothed.

2. Emerson said, "Converse with a mind that is grandly
simple, and all literature looks like word-catching."

3. In the metaphysical literature of today a good many
terms are used that are very confusing to those who have
not taken a consecutive course of lessons on the subject. It
seems to me wise to give here a clear, simple explanation
of two words frequently used, so that even the most
unlearned may read understandingly.

4. The words personality and individuality present distinct
meanings to the trained mind, but by the untrained mind
they are often used interchangeably and apart from their
real meanings.

5. Personality applies to the human part of you--the person, the external. Your personality may be agreeable or disagreeable to others. When you say that you dislike anyone, you mean that you dislike his personality--that exterior something that presents itself from the outside. It is the outer, changeable man, in contradistinction to the inner or real, man.

6. Individuality is the term used to denote the real man. The more God comes into visibility through a person the more individualized he becomes. By this I do not mean that one's individuality is greater when one is more religious. Remember, God is wisdom, intelligence, love, power. The more pronounced the manner in which any one of these qualities--or all of them--comes forth into visibility through a man, the greater his individuality.

7. Emerson was a man of large individuality, but retiring personality. He was grandly simple. He was of a shrinking, retiring nature (or personality). But just in proportion as the human side of him was willing to retire and be thought little of, did the immortal, the God in him, shine forth in greater degree.

8. John the Baptist represents the illumined intellect, the highest development of human conscioussness.

We may think of him as standing for personality, whereas Jesus typifies the divine self or individuality. John, recognizing the superiority of Jesus, said, "He must increase, but I must decrease" (Jn. 3:30).

9. One's individuality is that part of one that never changes its identity. It is the God self. It is that which distinguishes one person from another. One's personality may become

like that of others with whom one associates. Individuality never changes.

10. Do not confound the terms. One may have an aggressive, pronounced personality, or external man, which will, for a time, fight its way through obstacles and gain its point. But a pronounced individuality never battles; it is never puffed up; it is never governed by likes and dislikes and never causes them in others; it is God come forth in greater degree through a man, and all mere personality instinctively bends the knee before it in recognition of its superiority.

11. We cultivate individuality by listening to the "still small voice" (1 Kings 19:12) down deep within us, and boldly following it, even if it does make us different from others, as it surely will. We cultivate personality, in which live pride, fear of criticism, and all manner of selfishness, by listening to the voices outside ourselves and by being governed by selfish motives, instead of by the highest within us. Seek always to cultivate, or bring into visibility, individuality, not personality. In proportion as one increases, the other must decrease.

12. Whenever we fear a man, or shrink before him, it is because his personality, being the stronger, overcomes ours. Many timid persons go through life always feeling that they are inefficient, that others are wiser or better than they. They dread to meet a positive, self-possessed person; and when in the presence of such a one, they are laid low, just as a field of tall wheat is after a fierce windstorm has swept across it. They feel as though they would like to get out of sight forever.

13. All this, dear timid ones, is not because your fellow really is wiser or better than you, but because his personality--the external man--is stronger than yours. You never have a similar feeling in the presence of strong individuality. Individuality in another not only produces in you an admiration for its superiority, but it also gives you, when you are in its presence, a strange new sense of your own inherent possibilities, a sense that is full of exhilaration and comfort and encouragement to you. This is because a pronounced individuality simply means more of God come forth into visibility through a person, and by some mind process it has power to call forth more of God through you.

14. If you want to know how to avoid being overcome and thrown off your feet by the strong personality of others, I will tell you:

15. Always remember that personality is of the human and individuality is of God. Silently affirm your own individuality, your oneness with God, and your superiority to personality. Can God fear any person?

16. If you are naturally inclined to be timid or shrinking, practice of the following will help you overcome it. As you walk down the street and see anyone coming toward you, even a stranger to you, silently affirm such words as: "I am a part of God in visibility; I am one with the Father; this person has no power over me, for I am superior to all personality." Cultivate this habit of thinking and affirming whenever you approach any person, and you will soon find that no personality, however strong and aggressive, has the power to throw you out of the most perfect poise. You will be self-possessed because God-possessed.

17. Some years ago I found myself under a sense of bondage to a strong, aggressive personality with whom, externally, I had been quite intimately associated for several months. I seemed to see things through another's eyes; and while I was more than half conscious of this, yet I could not seem to throw it off. This personality was able, with very few words, to make me feel as if all that I said or did was a mistake, and that I was a most miserable failure. I was always utterly discouraged after being in this presence, and felt that I had no ability to accomplish anything.

18. After vainly trying for weeks to free myself, one day I was walking along the street, with a most intense desire and determination to be free. Many times before, I had affirmed that this personality could not affect or overcome me, but with no effect. This day I struck out farther and declared (silently of course), "There is no such personality in the universe as this one," affirming it again and again many times. After a few moments I began to feel wondrously lifted, and as if chains were dropping off. Then the voice within me urged me on a step farther to say, "There is no personality in the universe; there is nothing but God." After a short time spent in vigorously using these words, I seemed to break every fetter. From that day to this, without further effort, I have been as free from any influence of that personality as though it had never existed.

19. If at any time the lesser affirmation of Truth fails to free you from the influence of other minds, try this more sweeping one, "There is no personality in the universe; there is nothing but God," and you are bound to be made free.

20. The more you learn to act from the "still small voice" within you, the stronger and more pronounced will be individuality in you.

21. If you are inclined to wilt before strong personalities, always remember that God has need of you, through whom, in some special manner, to manifest Himself--some manner for which He cannot use any other organ--what need have you to quail before any person, no matter how important?

22. However humble your place in life, however unknown to the world you may be, however small your capabilities may seem at present to you, you are just as much a necessity to God in His efforts to get Himself into visibility as is the most brilliant intellect, the most thoroughly cultured person in the world. Remember this always, and act from the highest within you.

Lesson 8

Spiritual Understanding

Happy is the man that findeth wisdom,
And the man that getteth understanding.
For the gaining of it is better than the gaining of silver,
And the profit thereof than fine gold.
She is more precious than rubies:
And none of the things thou canst desire are to be compared
unto her.
Length of days is in her right hand;
In her left hand are riches and honor.
Her ways are ways of pleasantness,
And all her paths are peace.
She is a tree of life to them that lay hold upon her:
And happy is every one that retaineth her. . .
With all thy getting get understanding.
--Prov. 3:13-18; 4:7

1. What is this understanding on the getting of which
depends so much? Is it intellectual lore, obtained from
delving deep into books of other men's rocks (geology), or
stars (astronomy), or even the human body (physiology)?
Nay, verily, for when did such knowledge ever insure life
and health and peace, ways of pleasantness, with riches and
honor?

2. Understanding is a spiritual birth, a revelation of God
within the heart of man. Jesus touched the root of the
matter when, after having asked the apostles a question that
was answered variously, according to the intellectual
perception of the men, He asked another question to which
Peter gave a reply not based on external reasoning, but on

intuition. He said to Peter, "Blessed art thou, Simon Bar-Jonah: for flesh and blood hath not revealed it unto thee, but my Father who is in heaven" (Mt. 16:17).

3. You may have an intellectual perception of Truth. You may easily grasp with the mind the statement that God is the giver of all good gifts--life, health, love--just as people have for centuries grasped it. Or you may go further, and intellectually see that God is not only the giver, but the gift itself; that He is life, health, love, in us. But unless Truth is "revealed. . .unto thee" by "my Father who is in heaven" (Mt. 16:17), it is of no practical benefit to you or to anyone else.

4. This revelation of Truth to the consciousness of a person is spiritual understanding.

5. You may say to yourself, or another may say silently to you, over and over again, that you are well and wise and happy. On the mental plane a certain "cure" is effect, and for a time you will feel well and wise and happy. This is simply a form of hypnotism, or mind cure. But until, down in the depths of your being, you are conscious of your oneness with the Father, until you know within yourself that the spring of all wisdom and health and joy is within your own being, ready at any moment to leap forth at the call of your need, you will not have spiritual understanding.

6. All the teachings of Jesus were for the purpose of leading men into this consciousness of their oneness with the Father. He had to begin at the external man--because people then as now were living mostly in external things--and teach him to love his enemies, to do good to others, and so forth. These were external steps for them to take--a sort of lopping off of the ends of the branches; but they

were steps that led on up to the place of desire and attainment where finally the Master said, "I have yet many things to say unto you, but ye cannot bear them now" (Jn. 16:12).

7. He told them of the Comforter that should be in them, and which should teach them all things, revealing the "deep things of God" (1 Cor. 2:10) to them, showing them things to come. In other words, He told them how they might find the kingdom of heaven within themselves--the kingdom of love, of power, of life.

8. The coming of the Comforter to their hearts and lives, giving them power over every form of sin, sickness, sorrow, and over even death itself, is exactly what we mean by understanding or realization. The power that this consciousness of the indwelling Father gives is for us today as much as it was for those to whom the Nazarene spoke. Aye, more; for did He not say, "He that believeth on me, the works that I do shall he do also; and greater works than these shall he do" (Jn. 14:12)?

9. All the foregoing lessons have been stepping-stones leading up to the point where man may realize that ever-abiding inner presence of the Most High, God. "Know ye not that your body is a temple of the Holy Spirit which is in you?" (1 Cor. 6:19).

10. I cannot reveal God to you. You cannot reveal God to another. If I have learned, I may tell you, and you may tell another, how to seek and find God, each within himself. But the new birth into the consciousness of our spiritual faculties and possibilities is indeed like the wind that "bloweth where it will, and thou hearest the voice thereof, but knowest not whence it cometh, and whither it goeth; so

is everyone that is born of the Spirit" (Jn. 3:8). The new birth takes place in the silence, in the invisible.

11. Intellectual lore can be bought and sold; understanding, or realization, cannot. A man, Simon by name, once attempted to buy the power that spiritual understanding gives, from another who possessed it. "But Peter said unto him, Thy silver perish with thee, because thou hast thought to obtain the gift of God with money. Thou hast neither part nor lot in this matter: for thy heart is not right before God" (Acts 8:20,21).

12. Nor will crying and beseeching bring spiritual understanding. Hundreds of people have tried this method, and have not received that for which they earnestly but ignorantly sought. They have not received, because they did not know how to take that which God freely offered. Others have sought with selfish motives this spiritual understanding, or the power it would give them. "Ye ask, and receive not, because you ask amiss, that ye may spend it in your pleasures" (or to serve selfish ends) (Jas. 4:3).

13. Understanding, or realization of the presence of God within us, is as Peter said, "the gift of God" (Jn. 4:10). It comes to any and all who learn how to seek it aright. Emerson said, "This energy (consciousness of God in the soul) does not descend into individual life on any other condition than entire possession. It comes to the lowly and simple; it comes to whomsoever will put off what is foreign and proud; it comes as insight; it comes as serenity and grandeur. When we see those whom it inhabits, we are apprised of new degrees of greatness. From that inspiration (consciousness) the man comes back with a changed tone. He does not talk with men with an eye to their opinion. He tries them. . . .But the soul that ascends to worship the great

God is plain and true; has no rose color, no fine friends. .
.no adventures; does not want admiration; dwells in the
hour that now is."

14. "And ye shall seek me, and find me, when ye shall
search for me with all your heart" (Jer. 29:13). In that day
when, more than riches and honor and power and selfish
glory, you shall desire spiritual understanding, in that day
will come to you the revelation of God in you, and you will
be conscious of the indwelling Father, who is life and
strength and power and peace.

15. One may so desire a partial revelation of God within
himself, a revelation along one line--as, for instance, that of
health--as to seek it with all his heart.

And if he has learned how to take the desired gift, by
uncompromising affirmation that it is his already, he will
get understanding, or realization, of God as his perfect
health. So with any other desired gift of God. This is a step
in the right direction. It is learning how to take God by
faith for whatever one desires. But in the onward growth,
the time will come to every man when he will hear the
divine voice within him saying, "Come up higher," and he
will pass beyond any merely selfish desires that are just for
his own comfort's sake. He will desire good that he may
have the more to give out, knowing that as good (God)
flows through him to others it will make him "every whit
whole" (Jn. 7:23).

16. In the beginning of Solomon's reign as king over Israel,
the divine Presence appeared to him in a dream at night,
saying: "Ask what I shall give thee" (1 Kings 3:5). And
Solomon said: "Give thy servant therefore an
understanding heart" (1 Kings 3:9).

17. "And the speech pleased the Lord, that Solomon had asked this thing.

18. "And God said unto him, Because thou hast asked this thing, and hast not asked for thyself long life, neither hast asked riches for thyself, nor hast asked the life of thine enemies, but hast asked for thyself understanding to discern justice;

19. "Behold, I have done according to thy word: lo, I have given thee a wise and an understanding heart; so that there hath been none like thee before thee, neither after thee shall any arise like unto thee.

20. "And I have also given thee that which thou hast not asked, both riches and honor, so that there shall not be any among the kings like unto thee, all thy days" (1 Kings 3:10-13).

21. Thus in losing sight of all worldly goods and chattels, all merely selfish ends, and desiring above all things an understanding heart (or a spiritual consciousness of God within him as wisdom, life, power), Solomon received all the good or good things included, so that there was none among the kings like unto him in worldly possessions. "Seek ye first his kingdom (consciousness), and his righteousness; and all these things shall be added unto you" (Mt. 6:33). "For whosoever would save his life (the things of his life) shall lose it: and whosoever shall lose his life for my sake (that is willing to forget the so-called good things of this life for the Truth's sake, choosing before all things the finding of God in his own soul) shall find it" (Mt. 16:25).

22. When you first consciously desire spiritual understanding, you do not attain it at once. You have been living in the external of your being and have believed yourself cut off from God. Your first step after coming to yourself like the prodigal son is to say as he did, "I will arise and go to my Father" (Lk. 15:18) to turn your thoughts away from the external seeming toward the central and real; to know intellectually that you are not cut off from God, and that He forever desires to manifest Himself within you as your present deliverance from all suffering and sin. Just as Jesus taught, we begin our journey toward understanding by cutting off the branches of our selfishness. We try to love instead of to hate. Instead of avenging ourselves, we begin to forgive, even if it costs us great mental effort. We begin to deny envy, jealousy, anger, sickness, and all imperfection, and to affirm love, peace, and health.

23. Begin with the words of Truth that you have learned, and which perhaps you have as yet only comprehended with the intellect. You must be willing to take the very first light you receive and use it faithfully, earnestly, to help both yourself and others. Sometimes you will be almost overcome by questions and doubts arising in your own mind when you are looking in vain for results. But you must with effort pass the place of doubt; and some day, in the fullness of God's time, while you are using the words of Truth, they will suddenly be illumined and become to you the living word with you--"the true light, even the light which lighteth every man, coming into the world" (Jn. 1:9). You will no longer dwell in darkness, for the light will be within your own heart; and the word will be made flesh to you; that is, you will be conscious of a new and more divine life in your body, and a new and more divine love for all people, a new and more divine power to accomplish.

24. This is spiritual understanding. This is a flash of the Most High within your consciousness. "The old things are passed away, behold, they are become new" (2 Cor. 5:17). this will be the time when you will not "talk with men with an eye to their opinion." This is when you will suddenly become plain and true; when you will cease to desire admiration; when all words of congratulation from others on your success will fill you with an inexpressible sense of humility; when all mere compliments will be to you as "sounding brass, or a clanging cymbal" (1 Cor. 13:1). Truly, for that inspiration a man comes back with a changed tone!

25. With spiritual understanding comes new light on the Scriptures. The very Spirit of truth, which has come to bide with you forever in your consciousness, takes the deep things of God and reveals them to you. You will no longer run to and fro, seeking teachers or healers and rely solely on them for guidance. You will gladly let them help you reach the point where you will know that the living light, the living word within you, will "guide you into all the truth" (Jn. 16:13).

26. What we need to do is to seek the revelation of the living Christ within our own being, each for himself, knowing that only this divinity come forth can make us powerful and happy.

27. Every person in his heart desires, though he may not yet quite know it, this new birth into a higher life, into spiritual consciousness. Everyone wants more power, more good, more joy. And though to the unawakened mind it may seem that it is more money as money, or more goods that he wants, it is, nevertheless, more of good (God) that he craves; for all good is God.

28. Many today are conscious that the inner hunger cannot be satisfied with worldly goods, and are with all earnestness seeking spiritual understanding, or consciousness, of an immanent God. They have been seeking long, with a great desire of unselfishness and a feeling that when they have truly found God they will begin to do for others. Faithful service for others hastens the day-dawning for us. The gifts of God are not given in reward for faithful service, as a fond mother gives cakes to her child for being good; nevertheless they are a reward, inasmuch as service is one of the steps that leads up to the place where all the fullness of God awaits men. And while spiritual understanding is in reality a "gift of God," it comes to us more or less quickly in proportion as we use the light that we already have.

29. I believe that too much introspection, too much of what people usually call "spiritual seeking," is detrimental rather than helpful to the end desire--spiritual growth. "Spiritual seeking" is a sort of spiritual selfishness, paradoxical as this may seem. From the beginning to the end, Jesus taught the giving of what one possesses to him who has none.

30. "Is not this the fast that I have chosen (said the spirit of God through the prophet Isaiah): to loose the bond of wickedness, to undo the bands of the yoke, and to let the oppressed go free?

31. "Is it not to deal thy bread to the hungry, and that thou bring the poor that are cast out to thy house? when thou seest the naked, that thou cover him.

32. "Then shall thy light break forth as the morning, and thy healing shall spring forth speedily. . .

Then shalt thou call, and Jehovah will answer. . .Here I am.

33. "And if thou draw out thy soul to the hungry, and satisfy the afflicted soul; then shall thy light rise in darkness, and thine obscurity be as the noonday;

34. "And Jehovah will guide thee continually, and satisfy thy soul in dry places, and make strong thy bones; and thou shalt be like a watered garden, and like a spring of water, whose waters fail not" (Is. 58:6-11).

35. Stagnation is death. A pool cannot be kept clean and sweet and renewed unless there is an outlet as well as an inlet. It is our business to keep both the inlet and outlet open, and God's business to keep the stream flowing in and through us. Unless you use for the service of others what God has already given to you, you will find it a long, weary road to spiritual understanding.

36. We cry out and strain every nerve to obtain full understanding, just as sometimes we have heard earnest people, but people wholly ignorant of divine laws, beseech God for the full baptism of "the Holy Spirit" (Lk. 3:16) as in the day of Pentecost. Jesus said, "I have yet many things to say unto you, but ye cannot bear them now" (Jn. 16:12). We grow by using for others the light and knowledge we have. We expand, as we go on step by step in spiritual insight, until in the fullness of time--which means when we have grown spiritually up to the place where God sees that we are able to bear the many things--we receive the desire of our hearts, understanding.

37. Seek your own Lord. Take the light as it is revealed to you, and use it for others; and prove for yourselves whether there be truth in this prophecy of Isaiah, that "then shall thy

light rise in darkness, and thine obscurity be as the noonday" (Is. 58:10) and "then shall thy light break forth as the morning, and thy healing shall spring forth speedily" (Is. 58:8).

Lesson 9

The Secret Place of the Most High

1. There is nothing the human heart so longs for, so cries out after, as to know God, "whom to know aright is life eternal."

2. With a restlessness that is pitiful to see, people are ever shifting from one thing to another, always hoping to find rest and satisfaction in some anticipated accomplishment or possession. Men fancy that they want houses and lands, great learning or power. They pursue these things and gain them, only to find themselves still restless, still unsatisfied.

3. At the great heart of humanity there is a deep and awful homesickness that never has been and never can be satisfied with anything less than a clear, vivid consciousness of the indwelling presence of God, our Father. In all ages, earnest men and women who have recognized this inner hunger as the heart's cry after God have left seeking after things, and have sought, by devoted worship and by service to others, to enter into this consciousness; but few have succeeded in reaching the promised place where their "joy" is "full" (Jn. 16:24). Others have hoped and feared alternately; they have tried, with the best knowledge they possessed, to "work out" their "own salvation" (Phil. 2:12), not yet having learned that there must be an inworking as well as an outworking. "By

grace (or free gift) have ye been saved through faith; and that not of yourselves (nor of any human working), it is the gift of God, not of works, that no man should glory" (Eph. 2:8-9).

4. To him who "dwelleth in the secret place of the Most high," there is promised immunity from the "deadly pestilence" and "the snare of the fowler," from "the terror by night," and "the arrow that flieth by day" (Ps. 91); and even immunity from fear of these things. Oh, the awfully paralyzing effect of fear and evil! It makes us helpless as babes. It makes us pygmies, whereas we might be giants were we only free from it. It is at the root of all our failures, of nearly all sickness, poverty, and distress. But we have the promise of deliverance from even the fear and evil when we are in the "secret place." "Thou shalt not be afraid for the terror by night" (Ps. 91:5), and so forth.

"In the day of trouble he will keep me secretly in his pavilion: In the covert of his tabernacle will he hide me" (Ps. 27:5)." In the covert of thy presence wilt thou hide them from the plottings of man:

"Thou wilt keep them secretly in a pavilion from the strife of tongues" (Ps. 31:20).

5. The secret place! Why call a secret place? What is it? Where may we find it? How abide in it?

6. It is a secret place because it is a place of meeting between the Christ at the center of your being, and your consciousness--a hidden place into which no outside person can either induct you or enter himself. We must drop the idea that this place of realization of our divinity can be given to us by any human being. No one can come into it

from the outside. Hundreds of earnest persons are seeking, night and day, to get this inner revealing. They run from teacher to teacher, many of them making the most frantic efforts to meet the financial obligations thus incurred.

7. You may study with human teachers and from man-made books until doomsday; you may get all the theological lore of the ages; you may understand intellectually all the statements of Truth, and be able to prate healing formulas as glibly as oil flows; but until there is a definite inner revealing of the reality of an indwelling Christ through whom and by whom come life, health, peace, power, all things--aye, who is all things--you have not yet found "the friendship of Jehovah" (Ps. 25:14).

8. In order to gain this knowledge--this consciousness of God within themselves--many are willing (and wisely so, for this is greater than all other knowledge) to spend all they posses. Even Paul, after twenty-five years of service and of most marvelous preaching, said: "I count all things to be loss for the excellency of the knowledge of Christ Jesus my Lord. . .and do count them but refuse, that I may gain Christ" (or the consciousness of His divine self) (Phil. 3:8).

9. Beloved, that which you so earnestly desire will never be found by your seeking it through the mental side alone, any more than it has heretofore been found through the emotional side alone. Intuition and intellect are meant to travel together, intuition always holding the reins to guide intellect. "Come now, and let us reason together, saith Jehovah" (Is. 1:18). If you have been thus far on the way cultivating and enlarging only the mental side of Truth, as probably is the case, you need, in order to come into the fullness of understanding, to let the mental, the reasoning

side rest awhile. "Become as little children" (Mt. 18:3), and learning how to be still, listen to that which the Father will say to you through the intuitional part of your being. The light that you so crave will come out of the deep silence and become manifest to you from within yourself, if you will but keep still and look for it from that source.

10. And conscious knowledge of an indwelling God, which we so crave, is that of which Paul wrote to the Colossians, as "the mystery which hath been hid for ages and generations: but now hath it been manifested. . .Christ in you, the hope of glory" (Col. 1:26,27). "The secret place of the Most high" (Ps. 91:1), where each one of us may dwell and be safe from all harm or fear of evil, is the point of mystical union between man and Spirit (or God in us), wherein we no longer believe, but know, that God in Christ abides always at the center of our being as our perfect health, deliverance, prosperity, power, ready to come forth into manifestation at any moment we claim it. We know it. We know it. We feel our oneness with the Father, and we manifest this oneness.

11. To possess the secret of anything gives one power over it. This personal, conscious knowledge of the Father in us is the secret that is the key to all power. What we want is the revelation to us of this marvelous "secret." What will give it to us--who can give it to us except Him, the "Spirit of truth, which proceedeth from the Father" (Jn. 15:26)? Surely none other. That which God would say to you and do through you is a great secret that no man on the face of the earth knows, or ever will know except yourself as it is revealed to you by the Spirit that is in you. The secret that He tells me is not revealed to you, nor yours to me; but each man must, after all is said and done, deal directly with the Father through the Son within himself.

12. Secrets are not told upon the housetop; nor is it possible to pass this, the greatest of secrets, from one to another. God, the creator of our being, must Himself whisper it to each man living in the very innermost of himself. "To him that overcometh (or is consciously in process of overcoming), to him will I give the hidden manna, and I will give him a white stone (or a mind like a clean white tablet), and upon the stone a new name written, which no one knoweth but he that receiveth it" (Rev. 2:17). It is so secret that it cannot even be put into human language or repeated by human lips.

13. What you want today and what I want is that the words that we have learned to say as Truth be made alive to us. We want a revelation of God in us as life, to be made to our own personal consciousness as health.

We no longer care to have somebody just tell us the words from the outside. We want a revelation of God as love within us, so that our whole being will be filled and thrilled with love--a love that will not have to be pumped up by a determined effort because we know that it is right to love and wrong not to love, but a love that will flow with the spontaneity and fullness of an artesian well, because it is so full at the bottom that it must flow out.

14. What we want today is a revelation to our consciousness of God within us as omnipotent power, so that we can, by a work--or a look--"accomplish that which I please and it shall prosper in the thing whereto I sent it" (Is. 55:11). We want the manifestation to us of the Father in us, so that we can know Him personally. We want to be conscious of God working in us "both to will and to work" (Phil. 2:13), so that we may "work out" our "salvation" (Phil. 2:12). We have been learning how to do the

outworking, but have now come to a point where we must learn more of how to place ourselves in an attitude where we can each be conscious of the divine inner working.
15. Mary talked with the risen Jesus, supposing that He was the gardener, until suddenly, as He spoke her name, there flashed into her consciousness a ray of pure intuition, and in an instant the revelation of His identity was made to her.

16. According to the same sacred history, Thomas Didymus had walked daily for three years with the most wonderful teacher of spiritual things that has ever lived. He had watched this teacher's life and had been partaker of His very presence, physical and mental. He had had just what you and I have thus far received of mental training and external teaching. But there came a time when there was an inner revealing that made him exclaim, "My Lord and my God!" (Jn. 20:28). The secret name, which no other man could know for him, had that moment been given to him. There had come, in the twinkling of an eye, the manifestation to his consciousness of the Father in him as his Lord and his God. No longer simply our Father and our Lord, but my Lord and my God--my divine self revealed to me personally.

17. Is not this that which you are craving?

18. Each man must come to a time when he no longer seeks external helps, when he knows that the inner revelation of "my Lord and my God" to his consciousness can come to him only through an in-dwelling power that has been there all the time, waiting with infinite longing and patience to reveal the Father to the child.

19. This revelation will never come through the intellect of man to the consciousness, but must ever come through the

intuitional to the intellect as a manifestation of Spirit to man. "The natural man receiveth not (nor can it impart them) the things of the Spirit of God; for they are foolishness unto him; and he cannot know them, because they are spiritually judged" (1 Cor. 2:14), and they must be spiritually imparted.

20. In our eagerness we have waited upon every source that we could reach for the light that we want. Because we have not known how to wait upon Spirit within us for the desired revelation, we have run to and fro. Let no one misunderstand me in what I say about withdrawing himself from teachers. Teachers are good and are necessary, up to a certain point. "How then shall they call on him in whom they have not believed? and how shall they believe in him whom they have not heard? and how shall they hear without a preacher?" (Rom. 10:14).

21. Books and lectures are good, teachers are good, but you must learn for yourself that Christ, the Son of God, lives in you; that He within you is your light and life and all. When you have once grasped this beyond a doubt with the intellect, you cease looking to teachers to bring you spiritual insight. That Christ lives in you, Spirit itself must reveal to you. Teachers talk about the light, but the light itself must flash into the darkness before you can see the light.

22. Had the Master remained with the apostles, I doubt whether they would ever have gotten beyond hanging on His words and following in the footsteps of His personality.

23. Jesus knew that His treatments for spiritual illumination, given to His apostles from His recognition of Truth, would act in them as a seed thought, but He also

knew that each man must for himself wait upon God for the inner illumination which is lasting and real. God alone can whisper the secret to each one separately.

24. The inducement of power was not to come to them by the spoken word through another personality, not even through that of Jesus, with His great spiritual power and discernment. It was to come from "on high" (Is. 32:15) to each individual consciousness. It was the "promise of the Father, which. . .ye heard from me" (Acts 1:4). He had merely told them about it, but had no power to give it to them.

25. So to each of us this spiritual illumination that we are crying out after, this inducement of power for which we are willing to sell all that we have, must come from "on high," that is, to the consciousness from the Spirit within our being. This is the secret that the Father longs with an infinite yearning to reveal to each individual. It is because of the Father's desire within us to show us the secret that we desire the revelation. It is the purpose for which we come into the world--that we might grow step by step, as we are doing, to the place where we could bear to have the secret of His inner abiding revealed to us.

26. Do not be confused by seeming contradictions in the lessons. I have said heretofore that too much introspection is not good. I repeat it; for there are those who, in earnest desire to know God, are always seeking light for themselves, but neglect to use that which they already have to help others.

27. There must be an equal conscious receiving from the Father and giving out to the world, a perfect equilibrium between the inflowing and the outgiving, to keep perfect

harmony. We must each learn how to wait renewedly upon God for the infilling, and then go and give out to every creature that which we have received, as Spirit leads us to give, either in preaching, teaching, or silently living the Truth. That which fills us will radiate from us without effort right in the place in life where we stand.

28. In nearly all teaching of Truth from the purely mental side, there is much said about the working out of our salvation by the holding of right thoughts, by denials and affirmations. This is all good. But there is another side that we need to know a little more about. We must learn how to be still and let Spirit, the I AM, work in us, that we may indeed be made "a new creature" (Gal. 6:15), that we may have the mind of Christ in all things.

29. When you have learned how to abandon yourself to infinite Spirit, and have seasons of doing this daily, you will be surprised at the marvelous change that will be wrought in you without any conscious effort of your own.

30. It will search far below your conscious mind, and root out things in your nature of which you have scarcely been conscious, simply because they have lain latent there, waiting for something to bring them out. It will work into your consciousness light, and life, and love, and all good, perfectly filling all your lack while you just quietly wait and receive. Of the practical steps in this direction we will speak in another lesson.

31. Paul, who had learned this way of faith, this way of being still and letting the I AM work itself into his conscious mind as the fullness of all his needs was neither afraid nor ashamed to say:

32. "For this cause I bow my knees unto the Father, from whom every family in heaven and on earth is named, that he would grant you, according to the riches of his glory, that ye may be strengthened with power through his Spirit in the inward man; that Christ may dwell in your heart through faith; to the end that ye, being rooted and grounded in love, may be strong to apprehend with all saints what is the breadth and length and height, and depth, and to know the love of Christ which passeth knowledge, that ye might be filled unto all the fulness of God" (Eph. 3:14-19).

33. And then he gives an ascription: "Unto him that is able to do exceeding abundantly above all that we ask or think, according to the power that worketh in us" (Eph. 3:20).

Lesson 10

Finding the Secret Place

1. How to seek the secret place--where to find it--how to abide in it--these are the questions that today, more than at any other time in the history of the world, are engaging the hearts of men. More than anything else it is what I want. It is what you want.

2. All the steps that we are taking by speaking words of Truth and striving to manifest the light which we have already received are carrying us on swiftly to the time when we shall have consciously the perfect mind of Christ, with all the love and beauty and health and power which that implies.

3. We need not be anxious or in a hurry for the full manifestation. Let us not at any time lose sight of the fact

that our desire, great as it is, is only God's desire in us. "No man can come to me, except the Father that sent me draw him" (Jn. 6:44). The Father in us desires to reveal to us the secret of His presence, else we had not known any hunger for the secret, or for Truth.

4. "Ye did not choose me, but I chose you, and appointed you, that ye should go and bear fruit" (Jn. 15:16).

5. Whoever you are that read these words, wherever you stand in the world, be it on the platform preaching the gospel, or in the humblest little home seeking Truth, that you may make it manifest in a sweeter, stronger, less selfish life, know once and forever that you are not seeking God, but God is seeking you. Your longing for greater manifestation is the eternal energy that holds the worlds in their orbits, outpushing through you to get into fuller manifestation. You need not worry. You need not be anxious. You need not strive. Only let it. Learn how to let it.

6. After all our beating about the bush, seeking here and there for our heart's desire, we must come right to Him who is the fulfillment of every desire; who waits to manifest more of Himself to us and through us. If you wanted my love or anything that I am (not that I have), you would not go to Tom Jones or to Mary Smith to get it. Either of those persons might tell you that I could and would give myself, but you would have to come directly to me, and receive of me that which only I am, because I am it.

7. In some way, after all our seeking for the light and Truth, we must learn to wait, each one for himself, upon God for this inner revelation of Truth and our oneness with Him.

8. The light that we want is not some thing that God has to give; it is God Himself. God does not give us life or love as a thing. God is life and light and love. More of Himself in our consciousness, then, is what we all want, no matter what other name we may give it.

9. My enduement of power must come from "on high," from a higher region within myself than my present conscious mind; so must yours. It must be a descent of the Holy (whole, entire, complete) Spirit at the center of your being into your conscious mind. The illumination we want can never come in any other way; nor can the power to make good manifest.

10. We hear a great deal about "sitting in the silence." To many it does not mean very much, for they have not yet learned how to "wait. . .in silence for God only" (Ps. 62:5), or to hear any voice except external ones. Noise belongs to the outside world, not to God. God works in the stillness, and we can so wait upon the Father of our being as to be conscious of the still, inner working--conscious of the fulfillment of our desires. "They that seek Jehovah shall renew their strength" (Is. 40:31).

11. In one of Edward Everett Hale's stories, he speaks of a little girl who, amidst her play with the butterflies and birds in a country place, used to run into a nearby chapel frequently to pray; and after praying always remained perfectly still a few minutes, "waiting," she said, "to see if God wanted to say anything" to her. Children are often nearest the kingdom.

12. When beginning the practice of sitting in the silence, do not feel that you must go and sit with some other person. The presence of another person is apt to distract the mind.

Learn first how to commune alone with the Creator of the universe, who is all-companionship. When you are able to withdraw from the outside and be alone with Him, then sitting with others may be profitable to you and to them.

13. "Sitting in the silence" is not merely a sort of lazy drifting. It is a passive, but a definite, waiting upon God. When you want to do this, take a time when you can, for a little while, lay off all care. Begin your silence by lifting up your heart in prayer to the Father of your being. Do not be afraid that, if you begin to pray, you will be too "orthodox." You are not going to supplicate God, who has already given you things "whatsoever ye desire" (Mk. 11:24 A.V.). You have already learned that before you call He has sent that which you desire; otherwise you would not desire it.

14. You know better than to plead with or to beseech God with an unbelieving prayer. But spending the first few moments of your silence in speaking directly to the Father centers your mind on the Eternal. Many who earnestly try to get still and wait upon God have found that, the moment they sit down and close their eyes, their thoughts, instead of being concentrated, are filled with every sort of vain imagination. The most trivial things, from the fixing of a shoestring to the gossipy conversation of a week ago, chase one another in rapid succession through their minds, and at the end of an hour the persons have gained nothing. This is to them discouraging.

15. This is but a natural result of trying not to think at all. Nature abhors a vacuum, and if you make (or try to make) your mind a vacuum, the thought images of others that fill the atmosphere about you will rush in to fill it, leaving you as far away from the consciousness of the divine presence

as ever. You can prevent this by beginning your silence with prayer.

16. It is always easier for the mind to say realizingly, "Thy will is being done in me now," after having prayed, "Let Thy will be done in me." It is always easier to say with realization, "God flows through me as life and peace and power," after having prayed, "Let Thy life flow through me anew while I wait." Of course prayer does not change God's attitude toward us, but it is easier for the human mind to take several successive steps with firmness and assurance than for it to take one big, bold leap to a point of eminence and hold itself steady there. While you are thus concentrating your thoughts on God, in definite conversation with the author of your being, no outside thought images can possibly rush in to torment or distract you. Your mind, instead of being open toward the external, is closed to it, and open only to God, the source of all the good you desire.

17. Of course there is to be no set form of words used. But sometimes using words similar to the first few verses of the 103d Psalm, in the beginning of the silent communion, makes it a matter of face-to-face speaking: "Thou forgivest all mine iniquities (or mistakes); Thou healest all my diseases; Thou redeemest my life from destruction, and crownest me with loving kindness, now, now, while I wait upon Thee." Sometimes we may enter into the inner chamber with the words of a familiar hymn; as:

Thou art the life within me,
O Christ, Thou King of Kings;
Thou art Thyself the answer
To all my questionings.

18. Repeat the words many times, not anxiously or with strained effort, not reaching out and up and away to an outside God; but let the petition be the quiet, earnest uplifting of the heart to a higher something right within itself, even to "the Father in me" (Jn. 14:11). Let it be made with the quietness and assurance of a child speaking to his loving father.

19. Some persons carry in their faces a strained, white look that comes from an abnormal "sitting in the silence," as they term it. It is hard for them to know that God is right here within them, and while in the silence they fall into the way of reaching away out and up after Him. Such are earnest men truly feeling after God if haply they may find Him, when all the time He is near them, even in their very hearts. Do not reach out thus. This is as though a seed were planted in the earth, and just because it recognized a vivifying, life-giving principle in the sun's rays, it did nothing but strain and stretch itself upward and outward to get more of the sun. You can see at a glance that by so doing it would get no solid roots in the earth where God intended them to be. The seed needs to send roots downward while it keeps its face turned toward the sun, and lets itself be drawn upward by the sun.

20. Some of us, in our desire to grow, and having recognized the necessity of waiting upon God in the stillness for the vivifying and renewing of life, make the mistake of climbing up and away from our bodies. Such abnormal outstretching and upreaching is neither wise nor profitable. After a little of it, one begins to get cold feet and congested head. While one is thus reaching out, the body is left alone, and it becomes correspondingly weak and negative. This is all wrong. We are not to reach out away from the body even after the Son of righteousness. We are

rather to be still, and let the Son shine on us right where we are. The sun draws the shoot up as fast as it can bear it and be strong. We do not need to grow ourselves, only to let the Son "grow" us.

21. But we are consciously to let it; not merely to take the attitude of negatively letting it by not opposing it, but to put ourselves consciously where the Son can shine on us, and then "be still, and know" (Ps. 46:10) that while we wait there it is doing the work. While waiting upon God, we should, as much as possible, relax ourselves both mentally and physically. To use a very homely but practical illustration, take much the attitude of the entire being as do the fowls when taking a sun bath in the sand. Yet there is something more than a lax passivity to be maintained through it all. There must be a sort of conscious, active taking of that which God gives freely to us.

22. Let me see if I can make it plain. We first withdraw ourselves bodily and mentally from the outside world. We "enter into thine inner chamber, and . . . shut thy door" (Mt. 6:6) (the closet of our being, the very innermost part of ourselves), by turning our thoughts within. Just say, "Thou abidest within me; Thou art alive there now; Thou has all power; Thou art now the answer to all I desire; Thou dost now radiate Thyself from the center of my being to the circumference, and out into the visible world as the fullness of my desire." Then be still, absolutely still. Relax every part of your being, and believe that it is being done. The divine substance does flow in at the center and out into the visible world every moment you wait; for it is an immutable law that "every one that asketh receiveth" (Mt. 7:8). And substance will come forth as the fulfillment of your desire if you expect it to. "According to your faith be it done unto you" (Mt. 9:29).

23. If you find your mind wandering, bring it right back by saying again: "It is being done; Thou art working in me; I am receiving that which I desire," and so forth. Do not look for signs and wonders, but just be still and know that the very thing you want is flowing in and will come forth into manifestation either at once or a little farther on.

24. Go even beyond this and speak words of thanksgiving to this innermost Presence, that it has heard and answered, that it does now come forth into visibility. There is something about the mental act of thanksgiving that seems to carry the human mind far beyond the region of doubt into the clear atmosphere of faith and trust, where "all things are possible" (Mt. 19:26). Even if at first you are not conscious of having received anything from God, do not worry or cease from your thanksgiving. Do not go back of it again to the asking, but continue giving thanks that while you waited you did receive, and that what you received is now manifest; and believe me, you will soon rejoice and give thanks, not rigidly from a sense of duty, but because of the sure manifest fulfillment of your desire.

25. Do not let waiting in the silence become a bondage to you. If you find yourself getting into a strained attitude of mind or "heady," get up and go about some external work for a time. Or, if you find that your mind will wander, do not insist on concentrating; for the moment you get into a rigid mental attitude you shut off all inflow of the Divine into your consciousness. There must be a sort of relaxed passivity and yet an active taking it by faith. Shall I call it active passivity?

26. Of course, as we go in spiritual understanding and desire, we very soon come to the place where we want

more than anything else that the desires of infinite wisdom and love be fulfilled in us. "My thoughts are not your thoughts, neither are your ways my ways, saith Jehovah. For as the heavens are higher than the earth, so are my thoughts than your thoughts" (Is. 55:8).

27. Our desires are God's desires, but in a limited degree. We soon throw aside our limitations, our circumscribed desires (as soon, at least, as we see that more of God means more of good and joy and happiness), and with all our hearts we cry out in the silent sitting: "Fulfill Thy highest thought in me now!" We make ourselves as clay in the potter's hands, willing to be molded anew, to be "transformed into the same image" (2 Cor. 3:18), to be made after the mind of the indwelling Christ.

28. We repeat from time to time, while waiting, words something like these: "Thou art now renewing me according to Thy highest thought for me; Thou art radiating Thy very self throughout my entire being, making me like to Thyself--for there is nothing else but Thee. Father, I thank Thee, I thank Thee." Be still, be still while He works. "Not by might, nor by power, but by my Spirit, saith Jehovah of Hosts" (Zech. 4:6).

29. While you thus wait, and let Him, He will work marvelous changes in you. You will have a strange new consciousness of serenity and quiet, a feeling that something has been done, that some new power to overcome has come to you. You will be able to say, "I and the Father are one" (Jn. 10:30), with a new meaning, a new sense of reality and awe that will make you feel very still. Oh! how one conscious touch of the Oversoul makes all life seem different! All the hard things become easy; the troublesome things no longer have power to worry; the

rasping people and things of the world lose all power to annoy. Why? Because, for a time, we see as He sees. We do not have to deny evil; we know in that moment that it is nothing at all. We no longer rigidly affirm the good from sense of duty, but with delight and spontaneity, because we cannot help it. It is revealed to us as good. Faith has become reality.

30. Do not be discouraged if you do not at once get conscious results in this silent sitting. Every moment that you wait, Spirit is working to make you a new creature in Christ--a creature possessing consciously His very own qualities and powers. There may be a working for days before you see any change; but it will surely come. You will soon get so that you can go into the silence, into conscious communion with your Lord, at a moment's notice, at any time, in any place.

31. There is no conflict or inconsistency between this waiting upon God to be made perfect, and the way of "speaking the word" out toward the external to make perfection visible. Waiting upon and consciously receiving from the Source only make the outspeaking (holding of right thoughts and words) easy, instead of laborious. Try it and see.

32. Clear revelation--the word made alive as Truth to the consciousness--must come to every man who continues to wait upon God. But remember, there are two conditions imposed. You are to wait upon God, not simply to run in and out, but to abide, to dwell "in the secret place of the Most High" (Ps. 91:1).

33. Of course I do not mean that you are to give all the time to sitting alone in meditation and silence, but that your mind shall be continually in an attitude of waiting upon

God, not an attitude of clamoring for things, but of
listening for the Father's voice and expecting a
manifestation of the Father to your consciousness.

34. Jesus, our Master in spiritual knowledge and power,
had many hours of lone communion with the Father, and
His greatest works were done after these. So may we, so
must we, commune alone with the Father if we would
manifest the Christ. But Jesus did not spend all His time in
receiving. He poured forth into everyday use, among the
children of men in the ordinary vocations of life, that which
He received of the Father. His knowledge of spiritual
things was used constantly to uplift and to help other
persons. We must do likewise; for newness of life and of
revelation flows in the faster as we give out that which we
have to help others. "Go, preach. . .Heal the sick. . .freely
ye received, freely give" (Mt. 10:7,8), He said. Go manifest
the Christ within you, which you have received of the
Father. God works in us to will and to do, but we must
work out our own salvation.

35. The second indispensable condition to finding the
secret place and abiding in it is "my expectation is from
him":

"My soul, wait thou in silence for God only;

For my expectation is from him."

--(Ps. 62:5)

"Truly in vain is the help that is looked for from the hills,
the tumult on the mountains: truly in Jehovah our God is

the salvation of Israel" (Jer. 3:23). It is good that a man should both hope and quietly wait for the salvation of the Lord.

36. Is your expectation from Him, or is it from books, or teachers, or friends, or meetings, or societies?

37. "The King of Israel, even Jehovah is in the midst of thee" (Zeph. 3:15). Think of it; In the midst of you--at the center of your being this moment while you read these words. Say it, say it, think it, dwell on it, whoever you are, wherever you are! In the midst of you! Then what need for all this running around? What need for all this strained outreaching after Him?

38. "Jehovah thy God is in the midst of thee (not God in the midst of another, but in the midst of you, standing right where you are) a mighty one who will save; he will rejoice over thee with singing" (Zeph. 3:17). You are His love. It is you that He will rejoice in with singing if you will turn away from people to Him within you. His singing and joy will so fill you that your life will be a great thanksgiving.

39. Your Lord is not my Lord, nor is my Lord your Lord. Your Lord is the Christ within your own being. My Lord is the Christ within my own being.

40. There is one Spirit, one Father of all, in us all, but there are different manifestations or individualities. Your Lord is He who will deliver you out of all your troubles. Your Lord has no other business but to manifest Himself to you and through you, and so make you mighty with His own mightiness made visible; whole with His health; perfect by showing forth the Christ perfection.

41. Let all your expectation be from your Lord. Let your communion be with Him. Wait upon the inner abiding Christ often, just as you would wait upon any visible teacher. When you are sick "wait thou in silence for God only" (Ps. 62:5) as the Most High, rather than upon healers. When you lack wisdom in small or large matters, "wait thou in silence for God only," and see what marvelous wisdom for action will be given you. When desiring to speak the word that will deliver another from the bondage of sickness or sin or sorrow, "wait thou in silence for God only," and exactly the right word will be given you, and power will go with it, for it will be alive with the power of Spirit.

Lesson 11

Spiritual Gifts

1. It is very natural for the human heart first to set out in search of Truth because of the "loaves and the fishes" (Mt. 15:36).

2. Perhaps it is not too much to say that the majority of people first turn to God because of some weakness, some failure, some almost unbearable want in their lives. After having vainly tried in all other ways to overcome or to satisfy the want, they turn in desperation to God.

3. There is in the heart of even the most depraved human being, though he would not for worlds have others know it, an instinctive feeling that somewhere there is a power that is able to give him just what he wants; that if he could only reach that which to his conception is God, he could prevail on Him to grant the things desired. This feeling is itself

God-given. It is the divine self, though only a spark at the center of the man's being, suggesting to him the true remedy for all his ills.

4. Especially have people been led to seek Truth for the reward, "for the very works' sake" (Jn. 14:11), during the last few years, since they have come to know that God is not only able, but willing, to deliver them from all the burdens of their everyday life. Everyone wants to be free, free, free as the birds of the air--free from sickness, free from poverty, free from all forms of evil; and he has a right to be; it is a God-given right.

5. Thus far nearly all teaching has limited the manifestation of infinite love to one form--that of healing, Sickness, seemingly incurable disease, and suffering reigned on every side, and every sufferer wanted to be free. We had not yet known that there was willingness as there was power--aye, more, that there was intense desire--on the part of our Father to give us something more than sweet, patient submission to suffering.

6. When first the truth was taught that the divine presence ever lives in man as perfect life, and can be drawn on by our recognition and faith to come forth into full and abounding health, it attracted widespread attention, and justly so. Both teachers and students centered their gaze on this one outcome of a spiritual life, losing sight of any larger, fuller, or more complete manifestation of the indwelling Father. Teachers told all their pupils most emphatically that this knowledge of Truth would enable them to heal, and they devoted all their teaching to explanation of the principles and to giving formulas and other instructions for healing the body. Time has shown

that there are larger and broader views of the truth about spiritual gifts.

7. Healing of the body is beautiful and good. Power to heal is a divine gift, and as such you are fully justified in seeking it. But God wants to give you infinitely more.

8. Why should you and I restrict the limitless One to the bestowal of a particular gift, unless, indeed, we be so fairly consumed with an inborn desire for it that we are sure that it is God's highest desire for us? In that case we shall not have to try to heal. Healing will flow from us wherever we are. Even in a crowd of people, without any effort of our own, the one who needs healing will receive it from us; that one will "touch" (Mt. 9:21) us, as did the one woman in all the multitude jostling and crowding against Jesus. Only one touched Him.

9. Healing is truly a "branch" of "the vine" (Jn. 15:4), but it is not the only branch. There are many branches, all of which are necessary to the perfect vine, which is seeking through you and me to bear much fruit. What God wants is that we shall grow into such conscious oneness with Him, such realization that He who is the substance of all good really abides in us, that "ask whatsoever ye will, and it shall be done unto you" (Jn. 15:7).

10. If you are faithfully and earnestly living what Truth you know, and still find that your power to heal is not so great as it was at first, recognize it as all good. Be assured, no matter what anyone else says to you or thinks, that the seeming failure does not mean loss of power. It means that you are to let go of the lesser, in order that you may grasp the whole, in which the lesser is included. Do not fear for a moment to let go of just one little branch of divine power;

choose rather to have the highest thoughts of infinite mind, let them be what they may, fulfilled through you. We need to take our eyes off the ends of the branches, the results, and keep them centered in the vine.

11. You are a vessel for some purpose. If, when the time comes, you let go cheerfully, without humiliation or shame or sense of failure, your tense, rigid mortal grasp on some particular form of manifestation, such as healing, and "desire earnestly the greater gifts" (Cor. 12:31), whatever they may be in your individual case, you will be simply marvelous in the eyes of men. These works will be done without effort on your part, because they will be God, omnipotent, omniscient, manifesting Himself through you in His own chosen direction.

12. Paul said, "Now concerning spiritual gifts, brethren, I would not have you ignorant. . .Now there are diversities of gifts, but the same Spirit. . .For to one is given through the Spirit the word of wisdom; and to another the word of knowledge, according to the same Spirit: to another faith. . .to another gifts of healings. . .to another workings of miracles; and to another prophecy; and to another discernings of spirits: to another divers kinds of tongues; and to another the interpretation of tongues" (1 Cor. 12:1,4,8-10).

13. The same Spirit, always and forever the same, and one God, one Spirit, but in different forms of manifestation. The gift of healing is no more, no greater, than the gift of prophecy; the gift of prophecy is no greater than faith, for faith (when it is really God's faith manifested through us), even as a grain of mustard seed, shall be able to remove mountains; the working of miracles is no greater than the power to discern spirits (or the thoughts and intents of

other men's hearts, which are open always to Spirit). And "greatest of all these is love" (1 Cor. 13:13); for "love never faileth" (1 Cor. 13:8) to melt down all forms of sin, sorrow, sickness, and trouble. "Love never faileth."

14. "But all these worketh the one and the same Spirit, dividing to each one severally even as he will. For as the body is one. . .all the members of the body, being many, are one body; so also is Christ. . . .If the whole body were an eye (or gift of healing), where were the hearing? If the whole were hearing, where the smellig? . . .Ad the eye cannot say to the hand, I have no need of you." "But now hath God set the members each one of them in the body, even as it please him" (1 Cor. 12:11, 12, 17, 21, 18).

15. Thus Paul enumerates some of the free "gifts" of the Spirit to those who will not limit the manifestations of the Holy One, but yield themselves to Spirit's desire within them. Why should we fear to abandon ourselves to the workings of infinite love and wisdom? Why be so afraid to let Him have His own way with us, and through us?

16. Has not the gift of healing, the only gift we have thus far sought, been a good and blessed one, not only to ourselves, but to all with whom we come in contact?

17. Then why should we fear to wait upon God with a perfect willingness that the Holy Spirit manifest itself through us as it will, knowing that, whatever the manifestation, it will be good--all good to us and to those around us!

18. Oh, for more men who have the courage to abandon themselves utterly to infinite will--men who dare let go

every human being for guidance, and, seeking the Christ within themselves, let the manifestation be what He wills!

19. Such courage might possibly mean, and probably would mean at first, a seeming failure, a going down from some apparent success that had been in the past. But the going down would only mean a mighty coming up, a most glorious resurrection of God into visibility through you in His own chosen way, right here and now. The failure, for the time, would only mean a grand, glorious success a little later on.

20. Do not fear failure, but call failure good; for it really is. Did not Jesus stand an utter failure, to all appearances, when He stood dumb before Pilate, all His cherished principles come to naught, unwilling to deliver Himself, or to "demonstrate" over the agonizing circumstances of His position?

21. But had He not seemed to fail right at that point, there never would have been the infinitely grander demonstration of the Ressurection a little later on. "Except a grain of wheat fall into the earth and die, it abideth by itself alone: but if it die, it beareth much fruit" (Jn. 12:24). If you have clung to one spiritual gift because you were taught that, and you begin to fail, believe me, it is only the seeming death, the seeming disappearance, of one gift, in order that out of it may spring many new gifts--brighter, higher, fuller ones, because they are the ones that God has chosen for you.

22. Your greatest work will be done in your own God-appointed channel. If you will let Spirit possess you wholly, if you will to have the highest will done in you and through you continually, you will be quickly moved by it out of your present limitations, which a half success always

indicates, into a manifestation as much fuller and more perfect and beautiful as is the new grain than the old seed, which had to fall into the ground and die.

23. Old ways must die. Failure is only the death of the old that there may be the hundredfold following. If there comes to you a time when you do not demonstrate over sickness, as you did at first, do not think that you need lean on others entirely. It is beautiful and good for another to "heal" you bodily by calling forth universal life through you; but right here there is something higher and better for you.

24. Spirit, the Holy Spirit, which is God in movement, wants to teach you something, to open a bigger, brighter way to you. This apparent failure is His call to you to arrest your attention and turn you to Him.

"Acquaint now thyself with him, and be at peace:
Thereby good shall come unto thee."
--(Job 22:21)

Turn to the divine presence within yourself. Seek Him. Be still before Him. Wait upon God quietly, earnestly, but constantly and trustingly, for days--aye weeks, if need be! Let Him work in you, and sooner or later you will spring up into a resurrected life of newness and power that you never before dreamed of.

25. When these transition periods come, in which God would lead us higher, should we get frightened or discouraged, we only miss the lesson that He would teach, and so postpone the day of receiving our own fullest, highest gift. In our ignorance and fear, we are thus hanging on to the old grain of wheat that we can see, not daring to let it go into the ground and die, lest there be no

resurrection, no newness of life, nothing bigger and grander to come out of it.

26. Oh, do not let us longer fear our God, who is all good, and who longs only to make us each one a giant instead of a pygmy!

27. What we all need to do above everything else is to cultivate the acquaintance or consciousness of Spirit within ourselves. We must take our attention off results, and seek to live the life. Results will be "added unto" (Mt. 6:33) us in greater measure when we turn our thoughts less to the "works" and more to embodying the indwelling Christ in our entire being. We have come to a time when there must be less talking about Truth and teaching others to do so. There must be more incorporating of Truth in our very flesh and bone.

28. How are you to do this?

29. "I am the way, and the truth, and the life" (Jn. 14:6), says the Christ at the center of your being.

30. "I am the vine, ye are the branches: He that abideth (consciously) in me, and I in him (in His consciousness), the same beareth much fruit: for apart from me (or severed from me in your consciousness) ye can do nothing. . .If ye abide in me, and my words abide in you, ask whatsoever ye will, and it shall be done unto you" (Jn. 15:5,7).

31. I do assure you, as do all teachers, that you can bring good things of whatever kind you desire into your life by holding to them as yours in the invisible until they become manifest. But, beloved, do you not see that your highest, your first--aye, your continual--thought should be to seek

the abiding in Him, to seek the knowing as a living reality, not as a finespun theory that He abides in you? After that, ask what you will, be it power to heal, to cast out demons, or even the "greater works" (Jn. 14:12), and "it shall be done unto you" (Jn. 15:7).

32. There is one Spirit--"One God and Father of all, who is over all, and through all, and in all. But unto each one of us was the grace (or free gift) given according to the measure of the gift of Christ" in us (Eph. 4:6,7).

33. "For which cause I put thee in remembrance that thou stir up the gift of God, which is in thee" (2 Tim. 1:6).

34. Do not be afraid, "for God gave us not a spirit of fearfulness; but of power and love and discipline". (2 Tim. 1:7).

35. It is all one and the same Spirit. To be the greatest success, you do not want my gift, nor do I want yours; each wants his own, such as will fit his size and shape, his capacity and desires, such as not the human mind of us, but the highest in us, shall choose. Seek to be filled with Spirit, to have the reality of things incarnated in larger degree in your consciousness. Spirit will reveal to your understanding your own specific gift, or manner of God's desired manifestation through you.

36. Let us not desert our own work, our own God within us, to gaze or pattern after our neighbor. Let us not seek to make his gift ours; let us not criticize his failure to manifest any specific gift. Whenever he "fails," give thanks to God that He is leading him up into a higher place, where there can be a fuller and more complete manifestation of the divine presence through him.

37. And "I. . .beseech you to walk worthily of the calling wherewith ye were called, with all lowliness and meekness, with long suffering, forbearing one another in love; giving diligence to keep the unity of the Spirit in the bond of peace" (Eph. 4:1-3).

Lesson 12

Unity of the Spirit

1. Did we not know it as a living reality that behind all the multitude and variety of human endeavors to bring about the millennium there stands forever the master Mind, which sees the end from the beginning, the master Artist who Himself is (through human vessels as His hands) putting on the picture here a touch of one color and there a touch of another, according to the vessel used, we might sometimes be discouraged.

2. Were it not at times so utterly ridiculous, it would always be pitiful to see the human mind of man trying to limit God to personal comprehension. However much any one of us may know of God, there will always be unexplored fields in the realms of expression, and it is an evidence of our narrow vision to say: "This is all there is of God."

3. Suppose that a dozen persons are standing on the dark side of a wall in which are various sized openings. Viewing the scene outside through the opening assigned to him, one sees all there is within a certain radius. He says, "I see the whole world; in it are trees and fields." Another, through a larger opening, has a more extended view; he says: "I see trees and fields and houses; I see the whole world." The next one, looking through a still larger opening, exclaims:

"Oh! You are all wrong! I alone see the whole world; I see trees and fields and houses and rivers and animals."

4. The fact is, each one looking at the same world sees according to the size of the aperture through which he is looking, and he limits the world to just his own circumscribed view of it. You would say at once that such limitation was only a mark of each man's ignorance and narrowness. Everyone would pity the man who thus displayed--aye, fairly vaunted--his ignorance.

5. From time immemorial there have been schisms and divisions among religious sects and denominations. And now with the newer light that we have, even the light of the knowledge of one God immanent in all men, many still cling to external differences, so postponing, instead of hastening, the day of the millennium; at least they postpone it for themselves.

6. I want, if possible, to help break down the seeming "middle wall of partition" (Eph. 2:14), even as Christ, the living Christ, does in reality break down or destroy all misunderstanding. I want to help you to see that there is no real wall of difference between all the various sects of the new theology, except such as appear to you because of your circumscribed view. I want you to see, if you do not already, that everytime you try to limit God's manifestation of Himself in any person or through any person, in order to make that manifestation conform to what you see as Truth, you are only crying loudly: "Ho! everyone, come and view my narrowness and my ignorance!"

7. I want to stimulate you to lose sight of all differences, all side issues and lesser things, and seek but for one thing-- that is the consciousness of the presence of an indwelling

God in you and your life. And believe me, just as there is less separation between the spokes of a wheel the nearer they get to the hub, so you will find that the nearer you both come to the perfect Center, which is the Father, the less difference will there be between you and your brother.

8. The faith healer, he who professes to believe only in what he terms "divine healing" (as though there could be any other healing than divine), differs from the so-called spiritual scientist only in believing that he must ask, seek, knock, importune, before he can receive; while he of the Truth teaching knows that he has already received God's free gift of life and health and all things, and that by speaking the word of Truth the gifts are made manifest. Both get like results (God made visible) through faith in the invisible. The mind of the one is lifted to a place of faith by asking or praying; the mind of the other is lifted to a place of faith by speaking words of Truth.
9. Is there any real difference?

10. The mental scientist usually scorns to be classed with either of the other two sects. He loudly declares that "all is mind" and that all the God he knows or cares anything about is the invincible, unconquerable I within him, which nothing can daunt or overcome.

11. He talks about conscious mind and subconscious mind, and he fancies that he has something entirely different from the infinitely higher than either of the other sects. He boldly proclaims, "I have Truth; the others are in error, too orthodox," and thus he calls the world's attention to the small size of the aperture through which he is looking at the stupendous whole.

12. Beloved, as surely as you and I live, it is all one and the same Truth. There may be a distinction, but it is without difference.

13. The happy person who will from his heart exclaim, "Praise the Lord!" no matter what occurs to him, and who thereby finds that "to them that love God all things work together for good" (Rom. 8:28), is in reality saying the "all is good" of the metaphysician. Each one does simply "in all thy ways acknowledge him [or God, good]" (Prov.3:6), which is indeed a magical wand, bringing sure deliverance out of any trouble to all who faithfully use it.

14. The teachings of spirit are intrinsically the same, because Spirit is one. I heard an uneducated woman speak in a most orthodox prayer meeting some time ago. She knew no more of religious science than a babe knows of Latin. Her face, however, was radiant with the light of the Christ manifest through her. She told how, five or six years before, she had been earnestly seeking to know more of God (seeking in prayer, as she knew nothing about seeking spiritual light from people), and one day, in all earnestness, she asked that some special word of His will might be given directly to her as a sort of private message. These words flashed into her mind: "If therefore thine eye be single, thy whole body shall be full of light. . . .No man can serve two masters" (Mt.6:22-24).

15. She had read these words many times, but that day they were illumined by Spirit; and she saw that to have an eye "single" meant seeing but one power in her life; while she saw two powers (God and Devil, good and evil) she was serving two masters. From that day to this, though she had passed through all sorts of troublous circumstances--trials of poverty, illness in family, intemperate husband--she

found always the most marvelous, full, and complete deliverance out of them all by resolutely adhering to the "single" eye--seeing God only. She would not look even for a moment at the seeming evil to combat it or rid herself of it, because, as she said, "Lookin' at God with one eye and this evil with the other is bein' double-eyed, and God told me to keep my eye single."

16. This woman, who had never heard of any science, or metaphysical teaching, or laws of mind,

was combating and actually overcoming the tribulations of this world by positively refusing to have anything but a single eye. She had been taught in a single day by infinite Spirit the whole secret of how to banish evil and have only good and joy in her. Isn't it all very simple?

17. At the center, all is one and the same God forevermore. I believe that the veriest heathen that ever lived, he who worships the golden calf as his highest conception of God, worships God. His mind has not yet expanded to a state where he can grasp any idea of God apart from a visible form, something that he can see with human eyes and handle with fleshly hands. But at heart he is seeking something higher than his present conscious self to be his deliverance out of evil.

18. Are you and I, with all our boasted knowledge, doing anything more or different?

19. The Spirit at the center of even the heathen, who is God's child, is thus seeking, though blindly, its Father-God. Shall anyone dare to say that it will not find that which it seeks--its Father? Shall we not rather say it will find,

because of that immutable law that "he that seeketh findeth" (Mt.7:8)?

20. You have now come to know that, at the center of your being, God (omnipotent power) ever lives. From the nature of your relationship to Him, and by His own immutable laws, you may become conscious of His presence and eternally abide in Him and He in you.

21. The moment that any man really comes to recognize that which is absolute Truth--namely, that one Spirit, even the Father, being made manifest in the Son, ever lives at the center of all human beings--he will know that he can cease forever from any undue anxiety about bringing others into the same external fold that he is in. If your friend, or your son, or your husband, or your brother does not see Truth as you see it, do not try by repeated external arguments to convert him.

22. "And I, if I be lifted up from the earth, will draw all men unto myself" (Jn. 12:32). That which is needed is not that you (the human, which is so fond of talk and argument) try to lift up your brother. The Holy Spirit, or Christ within him, declares: "And I, if I be lifted up, will draw all men" (Jn. 13:32). You can silently lift up this I within the man's own being, and it will draw the man up unto--what? Your teaching? No, unto Christ, the divine in him.

23. Keep your own light lifted up by living the victorious life of Spirit. And then, remembering that your dear one, as well as yourself, is an incarnation of the Father, keep him silently committed to the care of his own divine Spirit. You do not know what God wants to do in him; you never can know.

24. If you fully recognize that the God that dwells in you dwells in all men, you know that each one's own Lord, the Christ within each one, will make no mistake. The greatest help that you can give to any man is to tell him silently, whenever you think of him: "The Holy Spirit lives within you; He cares for you, is working in you that which He would have you do, and is manifesting Himself through you." Then let him alone. Be at perfect rest about him, and the result will be infinitely better than you could have asked.

25. Keep ever in mind that each living person in all God's universe is a radiating center of the same perfect One, some radiating more and some less, according to the awakened consciousness of the individual. If you have become conscious of this radiation in yourself, keep your thought centered right there, and the Spirit of the living God will radiate from you in all directions with mighty power, doing without noise or words a great work in lifting others up. If you want to help others who are not yet awakened to this knowledge, center your thoughts on this same idea of them--that they are radiating centers of the All-Perfect. Keep your eye "single" for them, as did the uneducated woman for herself, and Spirit will teach them more in a day than you could in years.

26. Throughout the ages man has leaned to the idea of separateness instead of oneness. He has believed himself separate from God and separate from other men. And even in these latter days when we talk so much about oneness, most teachers of metaphysics manage again to separate God's children from Him by saying that while the child may suffer the Father knows no suffering nor does He take cognizance of the child's suffering; that we, His children, forever a part of Him, are torn and lacerated, while He,

knowing nothing of this, goes on as serenely and indifferently as the full moon sails through the heavens on a winter night.

27. It is little wonder that many, to whom the first practical lessons in the gospel of the Christ came as liberation and power, should in time of failure and heartache have turned back to the old limited belief of the Fatherhood of God.

28. There is no real reason why we, having come to recognize God as infinite substance, should be by this recognition deprived of the familiar fatherly companionship that in all ages has been so dear to the human heart. There is no necessity for us to separate God as substance and God as tender Father; no reason why we should not, and every reason why we should, have both in one; they are one--God principle outside of us as unchangeable law, God within us as tender, loving Father-Mother, who has compassion for our every sorrow.

29. There is no reason why, because in our earlier years some of us were forced into the narrow puritanical limits that stood for a religious belief, we should now so exaggerate our freedom as to fancy that we are entirely self-sufficient and shall never again need the sweet, uplifting communion between Father and child. The created, who ever lives, moves, and has his being in his Creator, needs the conscious presence of that Creator, and cannot be entirely happy in knowing God only as cold, unsympathetic Principle. Why cannot both conceptions find lodgment in the minds and hearts? Both are true, and both are necessary parts of a whole. The two were made to go together, and in the highest cannot be separated.

30. God as the underlying substance of all things, God as principle, is unchanging, and does remain forever uncognizant of and unmoved by the changing things of time and sense. It is true that God as principle does not feel pain, is not moved by the cries of children of men for help. It is a grand, stupendous thought that this power is unchanging law, just as unchanging in its control of our affairs as it is in the government of the starry heavens. One is fairly conscious of his entire being's expanding into grandeur as he dwells on the thought.

31. But this is not all, any more than the emotional side is all. True, there is law; but there is gospel also. Nor does gospel make law of no effect; it fulfills law. God is principle, but God is individual also. Principle becomes individualized the moment it comes to dwell in external manifestation in a human body.

32. Principle does not change because of pity or sympathy, even "as a father pitieth his children" (Ps. 103:13). The Father in us always moves into helpfulness when called on and trusted. It is as though infinite wisdom and power, which outside are Creator, Upholder, and Principle, become transformed into infinite love, which is Father-Mother, with all the warmth and tender helpfulness that this word implies, when they become focalized, so to speak, within a human body.

33. I do not at all understand it, but in some way this indwelling One does move to lift the consciousness of His children up and to place it parallel with God, Principle, Law, so that no longer two are crossed, but the two--aye, the three--the human consciousness, the individual father, and the Holy Spirit--are made one. In every life, with our present limited understanding, there come times when the

bravest heart goes down, for the moment, under the apparent burdens of life; times when the strongest intellect bends like a "reed shaken with the wind" (Mt.11:7), when the most self-sufficient mind feels a helplessness that wrings from it a cry for help from "the rock that is higher that I" (Ps. 61:2).

34. Every metaphysician either has reached, or must in the future reach, this place; the place where God as cold principle alone will not suffice any more than in the past God as personality alone could wholly satisfy. There will come moments when the human heart is so suddenly struck as to paralyze it, and for the moment it is impossible, even with strained effort, to think right thoughts.

35. At such times there will come but little comfort from the thought: "This suffering comes as a result of my wrong thinking; but God, my Father, takes no cognizance of it: I must work it out unaided and alone." Just here we must have, and we do have, the motherhood of God, which is not cold Principle any more than your love for your child is cold. I would not make God as Principle less, but God as individual more.

36. The whole business of your Lord (the Father in you) is to care for you, to love you with an everlasting love, to note your slightest cry, and to rescue you.

37. Then you ask, "Why doesn't He do it?" Because you do not recognize His indwelling and His power, and by resolutely affirming that He does now manifest Himself as your all-sufficiency, call Him forth into visibility.

38. God (Father-Mother) is a present help in time of need; but there must be a recognition of His presence, a turning

away from human efforts, and an acknowledgement of God only (a single eye) before He becomes manifest.

Lessons In Truth

Study Guide

Study Guide for students of Lessons in Truth

Lesson One

Bondage or Liberty, Which?

BIBLE--Deut. 3:22; Ps. 37:9; 125:1, 2; Jer. 39:18; Jn. 8:32

Questions on Bondage or Liberty, Which?

1. All suffering is the result of our belief that we are in
_____ to things of the flesh.

(see paragraph 1)

2. The Lord's statement "to me every knee shall bow"
means that human consciousness must _____
through various stages to the knowledge of oneness with
God.

(see paragraph 7)

3. God regards you not as His _____ but as His
_____.

(see paragraph 11)

4. The secret of power in living is _____.

(see paragraph 23)

5. Jesus daily went apart from the world so that He might return to it with renewed _____.

(see paragraph 29)

6. Prayer is when _____. Inspiration is when_____.

(see paragraph 30)

7. To forgive is to give some_____in return for evil given.

(see paragraph 32)

8. Failure to demonstrate may be caused by our harboring a spirit of_____.

(see paragraph 33)

9. God is present in every situation if we call His law into_____.

(see paragraph 34)

10. When there seems no way of escape from a situation, our prayer should be "_____ __ ___ ___."

(see paragraph 48)

PRAYER

I am unfettered, unbound, triumphant, glorious, splendid, free.

Lessons Two and Three

Statement of Being

Thinking

BIBLE--Ps. 4:8; Jer. 23:23, 24; Zeph. 3:17; Mt. 5:48; 23:9; Lk. 11:2; Jn. 4:24

Questions on Statement of Being

1. God is not a being or person. He is Spirit; He is the total of _____.

(see paragraph 5)

2. Man is the most complete_____of ___.

(see paragraph 15)

3. Mortal mind is the _____of_____.

(see paragraph 19)

4. There is no limit to God's readiness to give us the good we seek, if we are willing to __ ___ ____.

(see paragraph 23)

Questions on Thinking

1. Man is made up of three parts: _____, _____and_____.

(see paragraph 6)

2. There are two classes of Truth seekers; one requires that
every statement be _____, the other is willing to
"become as _____ _____."

(see paragraph 11)

3. The shortcut to spiritual understanding lies in seeking
directly the ____ ____of_____within.

(see paragraph 19)

4. Troubles and sorrows are the result of __ __. We
think wrongly because we are misinformed by our
_____.

(see paragraph 28)

5. God does not force us to think and act aright because this
would make us _____instead of _____.

(see paragraph 36)

6. If we are to receive more of God's good, we must
_____ good to those around us.

(see paragraph 42)

PRAYER

There is but one presence and one power in my life, God,
the good omnipotent.

Lessons Four and Five

Denials--Affirmations

BIBLE--Joel 3:10; Zeph. 3:15; Mt. 6:8, 11; 16:24; Lk. 9:23; Jn. 7:24; Rom. 8:38; 13:1

Questions on Denials

1. When Jesus said a man must "deny himself," He meant that we must deny the claims of ___ __ _____.

(see paragraph 10)

2. Denial is declaring not be true a thing that _____ ___.

(see paragraph 14)

3. If you repeatedly deny a false condition, it loses its ___ __ to make you unhappy. (see paragraph 17)

4. The first great denial is: "There is no ____." (It is suggested that the student commit the four great denials to memory.)

(see paragraphs 21-26)

Questions on Affirmations

1. Most persons first seek spiritual things because of _____ with their present conditions of life.

(see paragraph 1)

2. To affirm anything is to_____ ____ _____ that it is so, even in the face of _____.

(see paragraph 6)

3. The first great affirmation is: "God is life, love, intelligence, substance, omnipotence, omniscience, _____." (It is suggested that the student commit the four great affirmations to memory.)

(see paragraphs 13-23)

4. Denials have an _____ or ___ _____ tendency; affirmations_____ __.

(see paragraph 35)

PRAYER

I am Spirit, perfect, holy, harmonious. Nothing can hurt me or make me sick or afraid, for Spirit is God, and God cannot be sick or hurt or afraid. I manifest my real self now.

Lesson Six

Faith

BIBLE--Prov. 29:25; Mt. 9:29; 21:22; Mk. 11:22; Lk. 8:25; 17:5

Questions on Faith

1. "Faith is the _____of things hoped for, the _____of things not seen."

(see paragraph 4)

2. Blind faith is an _____ _____ in a higher power; understanding faith is based on immutable _____.

(see paragraph 12)

3. Intuition is the open end within one's own being of the _____ connecting each individual with God.

(see paragraph 14)

4. God is the _____ _____within every visible form of good.

(see paragraph 20)

5. The supply of every good awaits the _____, which must be made to call it forth.

(see paragraph 23)

6. The "promises of God" are certain statements that are always true, whether found in the _____ or in the _____.

(see paragraph 25)

7. When we ask God for anything there need not be any _____ or _____ about it.

(see paragraph 26)

8. Asking springs from _____ to possess some good.

(see paragraph 27)

9. Desire in the heart for anything is God's _____
sent beforehand that it is already ours.

(see paragraph 30)

10. We cannot actually desire what belongs to another; we
want the _____ of what his possessions stand for.

(see paragraph 37)

PRAYER

My faith is in God.

Lessons Seven and Eight

Personality and Individuality

Spiritual Understanding

BIBLE--Ps. 91:2; Mt. 5:16; Mk. 7:14; Lk. 6:19; 8:46; Jn.
3:30; 14:1, 26

Questions on Personality and Individuality

1. The more any person manifests true wisdom, the more
_____ are his ways of thinking and acting.

(see paragraph 1)

2. Personality applies to the _____ part of you;
individuality denotes the _____ _____.

(see paragraphs 5,6)

3. In the Bible, _____ ___ _____stands for personality; _____, for individuality.

(see paragraph 8)

4. You can be self-possessed in the face of the strongest personality if you are ___-_____.

(see paragraph 16)

5. If you are inclined to feel timid or inferior to others, remember that you are a _____ to God.

(see paragraph 22)

Questions on Spiritual Understanding

1. Understanding is a _____ _____, a revelation of God within the heart of man.

(see paragraph 2)

2. We begin our journey toward understanding by cutting off the branches of our _____.

(see paragraph 22)

3. With spiritual understanding comes new light on the _____.

(see paragraph 25)

4. _____ _____for others hastens the coming of our own dawn of understanding.

(see paragraph 28)

5. Too much introspection is _____ _____ to spiritual growth.

(see paragraph 29)

PRAYER

I trust God to establish that which is right, good, and orderly, because I know He is present in all persons and all situations.

Lessons Nine and Ten

The Secret Place of the Most High

--Finding the Secret Place

BIBLE--Ps. 91:1; Mt. 6:6, Jn. 8:12; 14:27; 16:13

Questions on The Secret Place of the Most High

1. The greatest desire of the human heart is to _____ ___.

(see paragraph 1)

2. "The "secret place" is our inner meeting place with the Christ, the place of _____ of our _____.

(see paragraph 6)

3. The secret of the key to all power is our _____, _____ _____ of the Father within us.

(see paragraph 11)

4. The "white stone" of the Bible represents a _____ like a clean tablet, on which our new spiritual name is written.

(see paragraph 12)

5. What we all want is that the words we have learned to say as Truth be made _____ to us.

(see paragraph 13)

Questions on Finding the Secret Place

1. The light we want is _____ _____.

(see paragraph 8)

2. "Sitting in the silence" is a passive, but a definite, _____ ____ ___.

(see paragraph 13)

3. The two conditions for receiving clear revelation are that we must abide in the "_____ _____," and our _____ must be from God. (see paragraphs 32,35)

4. We can prevent our mind from wandering by beginning our silence with _____.

(see paragraph 15)

5. While sitting in the silence we should _____ ourselves both mentally and physically.

(see paragraph 21)

PRAYER

The glory of the Christ consciousness, now awakened in my soul, quickens, illumines, and heals me.

Lessons Eleven and Twelve

Spiritual Gifts--Unity of the Spirit

BIBLE--Ps. 2:7, 8; 37:4; Isa. 64:4; Mt. 7:11; Jn. 4:10; 21:22; Rom. 6:23

Questions on Spiritual Gifts

1. The power of _____ is a great spiritual gift, but there are many more gifts.

(see paragraph 7)

2. Paul said that "there are _____ of gifts, but the same _____."

(see paragraph 12)

3. Our greatest work is done in our own _____ channel.

(see paragraph 22)

4. Failure is only the death of the ___ that new good may come.

(see paragraph 23)

5. In times of trial we need to get our attention away from ___ and seek to live the life.

(see paragraph 27)

Questions on Unity of the Spirit

1. All spiritual teachings are basically the same because Spirit __ ___.

(see paragraph 14)

2. With the "single" eye we see God only as the ___ _____in our life.

(see paragraph 15)

3. If others do not see Truth as we do, we should not try to convert them by repeated external _____.

(see paragraph 21)

4. There is no necessity for us to separate God as _____ and God as _____ _____.

(see paragraph 28)

5. God is principle but principle becomes _____ when manifested in the human body.

(see paragraph 31)

~~~~~~
~~~~~~~~~~~~~~~~~~~~~~~~~~~~

PRAYER

Because I work with the indwelling power of God, I reap
the perfect expression of His gifts in my life and affairs.

~~~~~~
~~~~~~~~~~~~~~~~~~~~~~~~~~~~~~

A Brief Glossary of Truth Terms

NOTE: The terms Truth (capitalized) and Unity are used to
designate the principles taught by the Unity School of
Christianity and presented to the public through its
literature. The term Truth (capitalized) means that which is
the fundamental and ultimate reality of anything. Truth may
transcend fact. For instance, to a Unity student a person's
illness is fact, not Truth; he believes that the Truth about
the person is wholeness; he believes that wholeness is
God's will for his children and that wholeness is the
fundamental and ultimate reality of each person's being.

Being--God; Diety.

being--finite existence.

consciousness--sum total of inner awareness.

demonstrate--to bring forth; reveal; prove.

demonstration--outward expression; proof.

Divine Mind--God.

manifest--to bring into form; to make evident to the senses;
prove; give evidence of.

manifestation--that which has been brought forth as evident to the senses; express.

meditate--to contemplate or ponder; to dwell in thought.

metaphysics--that division of philosophy which includes the science of being or reality, or the science of the fundamental causes and processes in things.

principle--basic law.

reality--that which is absolute or ultimately true.

realization--clear, vivid knowing; understanding.

the silence--state of stillness, relaxation, and receptivity wherein one may experience the presence of God.

Spirit--God; Deity.

spirit--life; the principle.

spiritual consciousness--inner or intuitive awareness of the things of Spirit.

substance--the spiritual essence out of which all things are made.